THE LITTLE PHOTOGRAPHER

A play
based on a short story by
Daphne du Maurier

DEREK HODDINOTT

SAMUEL FRENCH

LONDON
NEW YORK SYDNEY TORONTO HOLLYWOOD

© 1979 by du Maurier Productions Ltd

This play is fully protected under the Copyright Laws of the British Commonwealth of Nations, the United States of America and all countries of the Berne and Universal Copyright Conventions.

All rights, including Stage, Motion Picture, Radio, Television, Public Reading, and Translation into Foreign Languages, are strictly reserved.

No part of this publication may lawfully be transmitted, stored in a retrieval system, or reproduced in any form or by any means, electronic, mechanical, photocopying, manuscript, typescript, recording, or otherwise, without the prior permission of the copyright owners.

Rights of Performance by Amateurs are controlled by SAMUEL FRENCH LTD, 26 SOUTHAMPTON STREET, LONDON WC2E 7JE, and they, or their authorized agents, issue licences to amateurs on payment of a fee. **It is an infringement of the Copyright to give any performance or public reading of the play before the fee has been paid and the licence issued.**

Licences are issued subject to the understanding that it shall be made clear in all advertising matter that the audience will witness an amateur performance; that the names of the authors of the plays shall be included on all announcements and on all programmes; and that the integrity of the author's work will be preserved.

The Royalty Fee indicated below is subject to contract and subject to variation at the sole discretion of Samuel French Ltd

Basic fee for each and every
performance by amateurs   Code L
in the British Isles

In Theatres or Halls seating Six Hundred or more the fee will be subject to negotiation.

In Territories Overseas the fee quoted above may not apply. A fee will be quoted on application to our local authorized agent, or if there is no such agent, on application to Samuel French Ltd, London.

The Professional Rights in this play are controlled by Eric Glass Ltd, 28 Berkeley Square, London W1X 6HD.

> The publication of this play does not imply that it is necessarily available for performance by amateurs or professionals, either in the British Isles or Overseas. Amateurs and professionals considering a production are strongly advised in their own interests to apply to the appropriate agents for consent before starting rehearsals or booking a theatre or hall.

ISBN 0 573 11237 1

THE LITTLE PHOTOGRAPHER

First presented at the Everyman Theatre, Cheltenham on the 22nd March 1978, with the following cast of characters:

Madame la Marquise	Rosemary Leach
Edouard, the husband	Richard Simpson
Helene } the children	Lisa Rose
Celeste	Suzanne Wright
Miss Clay, the governess	Joan Morrow
Elise, the confidante	Jane Hilary
Monsieur Paul, the photographer	Tony Meyer
Therese, the sister	Anne Rosenfeld
Jean, the waiter	Geoffrey Snell

The play directed by Malcolm Farquhar

Setting by Donald Crosby

The action takes place in an hotel room overlooking the beach, somewhere in Northern France

Act I   Scene 1   Friday morning at about ten o'clock
           Scene 2   Three o'clock that afternoon
           Scene 3   Early afternoon, two weeks later
           Scene 4   Late afternoon, one week later
Act II Scene 1   Three days later
           Scene 2   The following morning

Time—the early 1900s

PRODUCTION NOTES

The set does not *have* to look large and opulent, but it must look elegant. Simplicity in its decoration therefore is desirable, with muted shades of colours giving the impression of space. The balcony could be part of the room with no French windows, indicating separation, but simplifying the setting. Only the barest of furniture is needed, so making this play particularly appropriate to the smaller stage.

The play does require subtlety in direction and acting to avoid falling heavily into melodrama. There should be a certain formality in the playing, with underlying tensions and passions just present. In other words, it should always have the veneer of respectability, hiding real human emotions—Marie's last entrance towards the end of Act One being a perfect example. Elise should not be too earthy, but played with a carefree disregard of the formalities of the period.

Therese should be played with evil dignity, and Monsieur Paul with boyish charm without concealing his strong masculinity.

The two children, Helene and Celeste, can be aged anywhere between 9 and 14, and while it is desirable to have two children, the play can, with certain changes in the dialogue, be presented with one child.

Derek Hoddinott

ACT I

Scene 1

An hotel room in northern France. Friday morning, about 10 o'clock

The hotel is a fashionable one and the room, which overlooks the beach, is elegant. While elegance is suggested, however, simplicity is the keynote, with muted colours predominating. On one side is a balcony, where potted plants decorate the balustrade. On it are four chairs of cane or wrought iron, and a small table. On the back wall of the room, which is slightly at an angle so that we are looking into the apex of the room, is a door leading to Marie's bedroom. Another door leads to the hall outside, and a third to the children's room. The furniture consists of a table or chiffonier with a mirror above it, a chaise-longue and matching chair, both of which have small ornate tables beside them, another chair, and a table with telephone. Most of the light that reaches the room comes from the balcony, therefore the emphasis of all lighting is on this side of the stage

As the Curtain rises the distant sound of the sea can be heard, fading gradually under the opening dialogue. The room is empty. A tray covered with a cloth is on the balcony table. It is going to be another hot day and the sun pours into the room, turning the white walls into a rich cream. The bedroom door stands open. Marie, Madame la Marquise, enters wearing a beautiful dressing-gown. She has just reached forty-two years of age. She is very attractive, slim and elegant, but her outward coolness disguises an inner turbulence and sensuality. She moves slowly on to the balcony and lifts the napkin covering the croissants. She begins to pour coffee. Suddenly she looks up and waves to her children playing on the beach below

Marie (*calling*) Hello, my darlings. We'll be down soon. (*Calling louder*) I said we'll be down soon. (*Suddenly*) Oh, Miss Clay! Miss Clay! See that Helene stays away from that rock pool. You know what happened last time. (*She waves again and continues to pour the coffee. She then puts down the pot and takes in a deep breath enjoying the fresh air. She then throws her children a kiss and returns to the room carrying her coffee cup*)

The bedroom door opens and Edouard appears. He is a man of forty-five. Very conservative in dress and behaviour. Even on holiday he is dressed in a neat suit and tie. He moves to the balcony and pours coffee

Edouard I wish you wouldn't shout, Marie.
Marie (*sitting on the chaise-longue*) Helene was near that deep rock pool. You remember what nearly happened last year.
Edouard (*pouring coffee*) No...
Marie (*almost to herself*) No, Edouard. You wouldn't.
Edouard What's that, my dear?

Marie I'm sorry, Edouard.
Edouard (*coming into the room*) Screaming from a third floor balcony is hardly seemly behaviour for someone in your position.
Marie I'll try and remember the next time our children are in danger of maiming themselves.
Edouard We employ a governess to protect the children, Marie. (*Looking at her as he sips his coffee*) And there's no need to pout. (*He eats a croissant*) You ought to have one of these. Delicious.
Marie I don't wish to eat. It's too hot.
Edouard Too hot? But it's only ten o'clock, my dear.
Marie I know, Edouard. How you can bear wearing a suit...
Edouard (*ignoring her remark*) Is that why you haven't dressed this morning? Because of the heat?
Marie I *am* dressed, Edouard.
Edouard *I* am dressed, Marie. You are not.

Marie gets up and moves away. Pause

I know you think I'm being tiresome....
Marie Very!

Marie drains her coffee cup and returns it to the balcony table. There is a long pause. Marie turns and looks at her husband momentarily

(*Sighing*) I'm sorry. (*Almost parrot-fashion*) Truly. I'm sorry. I do appreciate our position in society and it was inconsiderate of me to embarrass you. I apologize.
Edouard Now you're making fun of me.
Marie I was apologizing, Edouard.
Edouard You were mocking me. I could tell by the way you said it. I won't have it, Marie. Do you understand?
Marie If I was mocking you, Edouard—if—then it was because it's such a silly thing to argue about.
Edouard For you perhaps. Not me.

Marie turns away. There is a pause

Why don't you come and sit beside me so we may discuss the day's programme.
Marie (*hopefully*) Yes, I'd like to do that.
Edouard (*gently*) Very well then.

Marie sits beside Edouard. There is a pause, each waiting for the other to commence

Marie Well, Edouard. What do you suggest we do?
Edouard I—er—I thought you might have some bright ideas...
Marie I see. (*She looks away and sighs*) The truth is there *is* nothing we can do, today or any other day. We've been coming here for the last three years, to the same hotel, the same room, with the same view.
Edouard I thought you liked it here. That's why I didn't say anything.
Marie I thought *you* liked it. That's why *I* didn't say anything...

Act I Scene 1

Edouard Well, the children like it...
Marie (*irritated*) Oh, please, Edouard. Of course the children like it. Even I liked it for the first week but to spend a month here, a whole month, I don't think I could bear it again.
Edouard It's the heat that distresses you. Even for this part of France the weather's been exceptional this year.
Marie It's not the heat, though heaven knows it is overbearing...
Edouard (*looking at her*) Like me perhaps?

Marie sighs and places her hand on Edouard's knee

Marie (*gently, smiling*) No, darling. Not you. Me. I'm being unreasonable and rather boorish. When I consider how fortunate I am—how fortunate my children are—then I *am* being unreasonable. (*Pause*) Would you like another cup of coffee, Edouard?
Edouard Please—please.

Marie takes his cup and goes to the balcony table. She pours the coffee. As she does so her attention is caught by her children

Marie (*calling*) Celeste! Miss Clay! Look at Celeste...
Edouard (*standing*) Marie!!
Marie (*turning*) But Celeste is climbing...
Edouard (*angrily*) Please remember that Miss Clay is paid—*paid* to look after and if necessary to shout at the children. But I doubt even Miss Clay would shout from the third floor balcony in such an unseemly manner.

Edouard moves to the bedroom door and goes out

Marie sighs and comes back into the room. She is about to sit down when the telephone rings. She answers it

Marie Hello?...Yes this is she...Oh, yes, Monsieur Blanchard...Yes, my husband is here. One moment. (*She puts the receiver down, goes to the bedroom door and opens it*) Edouard. Monsieur Blanchard is on the phone from Paris...(*She moves to the chaise-longue and sits down irritably. She anticipates what is going to happen*)

Edouard comes in and picks up the receiver

Edouard Yes, Henri...Yes...How much is he offering?...That's absurd! There is no problem with that piece of land. Has he studied all the relevant papers?...(*He sighs*) Tomorrow? Didn't you tell him I was on holiday for another three weeks?...No, of course not...Well, I suppose if I left right away...(*He glances over at Marie, whose temper is mounting*) No—no, Henri, I appreciate you did what you could in my absence...(*He sighs*) Very well. I'll leave right away. Good-bye. (*He replaces the receiver and stands there for a moment. There is a silence*) I have to return to Paris.
Marie (*fighting back tears*) Oh?
Edouard (*moving down beside her*) I'm sorry, Marie.
Marie Always away somewhere. Meetings, negotiations...When we first got married it was different. (*Tearfully, inner desperation beginning to surface*)

Don't you understand, Edouard? I'm bored. Desperately bored. I want something to happen. To me. To our life together. I can't go on living as if I was—dying, Edouard, slowly dying.

There is a pause. Marie cries quietly. Edouard appears to be moved by her appeal, and comes and sits beside her

Edouard Marie. I understand how you feel believe me. I too have felt the same...
Marie You have your work as consolation.
Edouard But you have the children.
Marie (*sadly, looking at him*) Oh, Edouard, you don't understand, you don't...
Edouard I do, Marie. You want change, excitement...
Marie I want to feel alive, Edouard. That's all. Alive.

Edouard looks momentarily at her, then kisses her cheek

Edouard You shall, my dear. I promise. We'll try to be more tolerant of each other.
Marie Edouard! Convince me you mean it.

Edouard takes Marie into his arms and kisses her—with little passion

Edouard I must go to Paris now. But when I return we'll make plans for the future. We'll change our lives. We won't come here again, for a start. And I'll—I'll buy a yacht. Now what do you think of that?
Marie A yacht?
Edouard We can go wherever you want. Have parties on board. Make new friends, younger, exciting friends...
Marie Oh, Edouard! (*She kisses his cheek*)
Edouard (*getting up*) I'll telephone you every day. I promise. (*Going to the bedroom*) I must get the papers I brought with me. There's plenty of money in the deposit box downstairs. I'll inform the Manager you're to have access to it during my absence.

Edouard exits to the bedroom

Marie Aren't you packing any clothes?
Edouard (*off*) I have all I need in Paris.

Marie gets up and moves slowly to the bedroom door

Marie (*calling*) Edouard.
Edouard (*off*) Yes?
Marie Something good has come out of this morning hasn't it?
Edouard (*off*) I hope so, my dear.

Edouard enters with his briefcase

I hope so. Say good-bye to the children for me.
Marie They'll be so disappointed.
Edouard (*kissing her*) I'll telephone you as soon as I get to Paris. Good-bye, my darling...

Act I Scene 1

Marie Good-bye, Edouard. And please hurry back...
Edouard Two days at the most. I promise.
Marie (*suddenly*) Oh! The photograph!
Edouard What photograph?
Marie We were having a family portrait taken this afternoon. Here. We arranged it—at least I arranged it at that little shop in the village. You remember? I told you.
Edouard Oh, yes. Well, you can still have it taken if you want to. You and the children.
Marie Then I shouldn't cancel it?
Edouard No. It'll pass a pleasant hour or two. Good-bye, darling.
Marie Good-bye, Edouard.

She hugs and kisses him passionately on the lips. He gently struggles free

Edouard (*gently and slightly embarrassed*) Good-bye, Marie.

Marie's expression changes from delight to helplessness. As he moves to the hall door it is clear he has not changed. And neither has she.

   Edouard exits

When he has gone she stands alone in the centre of the room looking at the closed door. Then slowly she looks around the room feeling her isolation. Suddenly she sees herself in the mirror above the chiffonier and moves towards it. She stands in front of it looking at her features. Then slowly, with her back to the audience, she unwraps her dressing gown and lowers it from her shoulders so that we can see her naked back. She stands there momentarily admiring herself

   There is a timid knock on the door, which immediately opens, admitting a young waiter

The Marquise becomes acutely embarrassed. The waiter mumbles profuse apologies and is about to withdraw when Marie hurriedly lifts the gown to cover her shoulders and then turns on the waiter

Marie How dare you come in without being asked!
Waiter Please, Madame—I'm sorry...
Marie This is a private room...
Waiter My apologies, Madame la Marquise.
Marie I shall have to speak to the Manager. You didn't even knock.
Waiter I did knock, Madame.
Marie I didn't hear you.
Waiter I did knock, Madame, I assure you.
Marie You should have waited then.
Waiter Yes, Madame, I realize that...
Marie Or knocked louder. (*She looks at the poor trembling Waiter and moves towards the balcony*) What is it you want?
Waiter I—I came to see if you had finished with the breakfast tray, Madame.
Marie (*indicating the balcony*) It's out there.

Pause. He does not move. Marie turns

Well?

Waiter May I—may I take it then, Madame la Marquise?

Marie Yes.

The Waiter moves to the balcony, having to pass Marie as he does so. Suddenly the telephone rings and Marie goes to the phone while the Waiter collects the breakfast things on to the tray

Hello... Who?... Yes... Who did you say you were? (*Excitedly*) Elise Mannon. I don't believe it. Are you the same Elise...? But this is marvellous, it must be twenty years... Where are you?... What?... Downstairs? Good heavens! But I'm not dressed yet... I know. Come up here instead. I have nothing to do... We can talk as long as we like. Room one hundred and four. Third floor. Hurry, Elise. I can't wait to see you again.

Marie replaces the receiver as the Waiter makes for the door. Marie blocks his exit

Waiter (*nervously*) Once again, Madame, I humbly apologize.

Marie (*softening her attitude*) I'm pleased to hear it. Perhaps I won't speak to the Manager—this time.

Waiter (*bowing stiffly*) Thank you, Madame.

He moves to go out but Marie prevents it

Marie (*moving closer to him*) How long have you been employed here?

Waiter Only three months, Madame la Marquise.

Marie Clearly you have a great deal to learn.

Waiter Yes, Madame.

Marie What is your name?

Waiter Jean, Madame.

Marie How old?

Waiter Twenty-one, Madame la Marquise.

Marie Twenty-one. (*Looking straight at him*) What a temptation life must be at twenty-one.

She moves around eyeing him like a stallion at an auction. He stands there holding the tray, feeling vulnerable. He gulps

Well young man... Well, Jean...

Waiter Yes, Madame...

Marie You had better go, hadn't you?

Waiter Yes, Madame la Marquise. Thank you.

He goes to the door, trembling. When he reaches it, he negotiates it with difficulty. Marie watches him, trying to conceal her mirth

The Waiter exits

Marie has so much enjoyed this minor encounter that when the door closes she allows herself to laugh out loud. She then goes to the mirror and adjusts her hair. There is a knock. She hurries to the door and opens it

Elise stands there. She is about the same age as Marie. She has married well,

Act I Scene 1

but retains an open sense of humour. She is a gay, carefree person who likes to shock people by her subtle abandoned behaviour. She must be played with sophistication as her position demands

Marie Elise!
Elise Marie! Marie, my darling...

There is a flurry of kisses and embraces

Marie It's wonderful seeing you again after all this time. Come in. Come in...

Marie closes the door

Elise It was luck, I assure you—simply luck.
Marie You look wonderful. Still so young. Please. Sit down. How did you discover me here?
Elise I saw your name in the hotel register. They were searching for the key to my room. It was on the wrong hook or something. Anyway, while they were looking for it I took the liberty of browsing through the register to see what kind of company I was keeping when I saw your name. Mind you, I knew you'd married well. It was reported in the society columns, so you can imagine how I felt when I saw the name staring up at me. I decided to phone you right away.
Marie Well, I'm glad you did. Tell me, Elise. Are you married?
Elise Yes.
Marie And where is your husband now?
Elise Downstairs in the conservatory, reading the morning paper.
Marie I look forward to meeting him.
Elise And Monsieur le Marquis?
Marie He's just left for Paris.
Elise Paris?
Marie He was called away on urgent business.
Elise In the middle of a holiday?
Marie Yes.
Elise And you're left here alone?
Marie Not quite alone. I have two children. Celeste and Helene.
Elise Where are they? I'd love to see them.
Marie They're down on the beach with Miss Clay, their governess.
Elise No boys, then?
Marie No. (*Seriously*) I think Edouard is a little disappointed in me.
Elise Disappointed in you? Nonsense!
Marie Have you any children?
Elise I lost my first child. I can't have any more.
Marie Oh, I'm sorry.
Elise (*changing the subject*) It doesn't worry me. Nor Phillipe. He's a doctor— a rather important specialist.
Marie Oh? How exciting.
Elise Not really. In fact it's rather boring. I think I married the most boring man in France. At least for a woman like me. Phillipe is attached to hypodermic needles and the odour of chloroform. I tell you something, Marie. If

I ever return to this earth I'm coming back as a man. They have all the fun. The awful thing is that Phillipe loves me in his own quiet way and I love him—from a distance. I have all the money I need, all the clothes I can buy, but what does it all mean if you don't well, *feel* married—act married.

There is an awkward pause

You know something, Marie?

Marie looks at her

I believe we're in the same boat.
Marie What do you mean?
Elise Like me—you're married to a bore!
Marie Elise! (*She moves and sits next to Elise*)

They start to laugh together, in a common bond

Elise I knew I was right! As soon as you told me your husband had returned to Paris I knew it. Any man who finds business more rewarding than a woman can't be anything else *but* a bore.
Marie (*continuing to laugh*) You're an unsettling influence. You haven't been here five minutes and already I feel...
Elise What?
Marie Er... (*Standing*) I'm sure you'd like some coffee. (*Moving to the phone*) I'll have a tray brought up. (*Picking up the receiver and waiting*) I shouldn't say this, Elise, but your frankness is like a breath of fresh air to me... (*On the phone*) Hello... Yes—would you send up a tray of coffee and biscuits to my room please... One hundred and four... Thank you. (*She replaces the receiver*)
Elise So? What are you going to do about it?
Marie What can one do?
Elise What any sensible, attractive woman does. You make your own arrangements.
Marie (*after a pause*) My own arrangements?
Elise (*realizing she might have gone too far*) Oh, I shouldn't have said that. I'm sorry.
Marie (*thoughtfully*) No. No. It's all right. Truly.
Elise Clearly you and I live in different worlds, Marie. I forgot.
Marie Yes. But it makes me wonder who has the better bargain.
Elise How can you say that? You have two beautiful children...
Marie I hardly see them. Miss Clay takes care of them. Edouard prefers it that way.
Elise Oh. (*Pause*) So—what do you do with yourself all day?
Marie I paint—read...

Marie looks up and sees Elise looking at her

Elise (*deliberately changing the subject*) How long are you here for?
Marie Another three weeks.
Elise So am I.
Marie Oh, that's wonderful! We can see each other every day...

Act I Scene 1

Elise Until Monsieur le Marquis returns. I don't think he'd approve of someone like me.

There is a gentle tapping on the door

Marie Come in.

The door opens and the young Waiter comes in with a tray of coffee

Ah. Coffee. Put it here will you? (*Indicating the small table beside the chaise*) Thank you—Jean.
Waiter Will that be all, Madame la Marquise?
Marie Yes, thank you. You may go.
Waiter Thank you, Madame.

The Waiter leaves

Elise watches him go

Elise Why don't we have waiters like that on our floor, I wonder.
Marie (*pouring coffee*) Milk and sugar?
Elise Please. (*She watches Marie*)

Marie senses Elise looking at her. She hands her the cup

Thank you.

Marie pours her own coffee

Marie (*tentatively*) You said a moment ago—about making one's own arrangements...
Elise It was nothing, Marie.

Marie looks at her, waiting

Well, perhaps I'm ahead of my time. I don't know—but why should I, because I happen to be a woman, refrain from enjoying life—to the full...
Marie What is your answer to the problem? (*She sips her coffee*)
Elise A lover.

Marie nearly chokes. Elise bursts into laughter

A lover. That's what you should have. That's what you *need*. Take a lover, Marie. You can't sit here in this room for the next three weeks alone. You'll go mad.
Marie Elise—I—I couldn't do that.
Elise Why not? If your husband had the slightest consideration for you...
Marie Have you?
Elise Have I what?
Marie Taken a lover.
Elise Of course. He's twenty-five and his name is Gerard. As a result Phillipe is happy and I'm happy. I make no demands on him and he none on me.
Marie And he doesn't suspect?
Elise We're very discreet.

Marie gets up and moves to the balcony

(*Looking after her*) Of course, it's different when you have children.
Marie (*turning, seriously*) Yes. There are the children to consider. (*Smiling*) I'm quite breathless, Elise. You come here with all these advanced ideas about intimate relationships outside marriage—it's taken me by storm...
Elise Has it? Remember we were at school together, Marie. Even then we were branded as undisciplined. And why? Because we had that inner spark, that capacity to enjoy life—not waste it. Are you telling me you've changed? That the spirit has gone?
Marie It's all right to feel that way when you're young. But maturity, position bring responsibilities...
Elise Marie, my dear, you also have a responsibility to yourself. Don't let other people live your life for you. I saw the way you looked at that waiter just now...
Marie (*taken aback*) What do you mean?
Elise You wanted him.
Marie Elise!
Elise You *wanted* him, Marie. Don't try and deny it.
Marie A mere boy!
Elise A young man—a vigorous body...
Marie *Stop it!* (*Pause*) He's a servant. You don't think I'd have an affair with a servant.
Elise What does it matter as long as you're happy.
Marie You make it all sound so matter-of-fact...
Elise It is.
Marie No. It's romance I need.
Elise It's sex you need, Marie.
Marie (*angrily*) I won't have you talk like that!

Marie moves further out on to the balcony. Pause

Elise I'm sorry. (*Pause*) But Marie—you must have met at least *one* nice man since you've been here.

Pause

Marie (*turning*) Many *nice* young men, yes, but none...
Elise There must be *one*. One man whom you'd like—to know a little better—hm?

Pause

Marie (*moving back to the chaise-longue*) Well, yes—one, perhaps. He's a photographer. He owns a small shop in the village. I took in some film to be developed and there he was. Standing behind the counter.
Elise How old?
Marie In his twenties. His name is Monsieur Paul. He's coming here this afternoon.
Elise Here? Really?
Marie Yes. He's coming to take our photograph that's all. The girls and I.

The Lights fade to BLACKOUT

Act I Scene 2

Scene 2

The same. Three o'clock that afternoon

The richness of the sun has now coloured the room gold. As the lights come up Celeste and Helene are sitting on the chaise-longue like two dolls. Both are dressed in neat pretty frocks with bows in their hair. Through the bedroom door comes Miss Clay. She is about thirty, not unattractive but a little prim. She is birdlike in her mannerisms. She has a genuine rapport with the children, however

Miss Clay Celeste. Have you got a handkerchief?
Celeste (*checking*) It's here, Miss Clay.
Miss Clay What about you, Helene?
Helene (*doing the same*) Here, Miss Clay.
Miss Clay Good. Now I want you to sit there until your mama comes out to look at you. Helene.
Helene Yes, Miss Clay.
Miss Clay You have a smudge on your cheek. Your left cheek. Just below the eye.

Helene takes out her handkerchief and rubs her cheek strongly

Don't scrub. You'll leave a red mark. Gently. A lady always does everything gently. You never see your mama behave with anything but poise and elegance, do you?
Helene No, Miss Clay.
Celeste Can I have a photograph taken on my own, Miss Clay?
Miss Clay Your mama will decide that. Not I.
Helene If Celeste is having her photograph taken on her own so am I. It's not fair if she...
Miss Clay Your mama will decide so there is no point in squabbling about it.
Celeste I wish Papa hadn't gone back to Paris. It would have been nice having him in the picture.
Miss Clay Your papa has to work very hard so you can have lovely long holidays by the sea.
Helene It was such fun when he was on the beach with us yesterday.
Miss Clay Well, I'm sure he's as disappointed as you not to be here.

The bedroom door opens and Marie comes in. She looks very beautiful in a white lace dress. Her hair is beautifully done and she personifies the elegance and poise Miss Clay referred to earlier

Madame...
Marie (*to the children*) Are you all ready, my darlings? Let me look at you.
Helene You look beautiful, Mama. Doesn't she, Celeste?
Marie Thank you, Helene.
Celeste You look like an angel, Mama.

Marie (*smiling*) Oh, I don't think that's true. There's nothing angelic about me, I'm afraid.

Miss Clay The children are right, Madame la Marquise. You do look beautiful. If I may say so.

Marie Thank you, Miss Clay. Please sit down.

Miss Clay sits

(*To the children*) Now let me see. Stand up both of you.

Helene and Celeste stand up and move slightly downstage. Marie starts to walk round them

Celeste This is what the soldiers do, isn't it, Mama?

Marie That's right. Inspection. Seeing that they're smart, well groomed and a credit to their Regiment and their Commanding Officer.

Helene And are we a credit to you, Mama?

Marie (*smiling*) I think you'll pass. (*She gives them a kiss each*). Now sit down.

Helene and Celeste sit

Miss Clay Do they meet with your approval, Madame?

Marie They do, Miss Clay. Excellent, in fact. Now, let me see. What time is it? (*She looks at her pendant watch*) It's five past three. The photographer's late.

Miss Clay He must have been delayed. I'm sure such a discourtesy is unintentional.

Marie So am I, Miss Clay. (*To the children*) Now, children. You'd better go and wait in your room until Miss Clay calls you. I think that would be best, don't you?

Miss Clay As you say, Madame.

Marie Then off you go.

Celeste and Helene move to the door, shepherded by Miss Clay

And don't roll all over the beds. I want you looking like that when the photographer arrives.

Celeste ⎫
Helene ⎭ (*very bored, and showing it*) Yes, Mama. ⎧ *Speaking*
⎩ *together*

Miss Clay (*opening the door*) I'll wait with the children, Madame.

Marie No—er, Miss Clay, I'd prefer it if you remained with me until he comes.

Miss Clay Very well, Madame. (*To the children*) Go into your room, children, and stay there quietly until it is time for me to call you.

Celeste and Helene exit to their room, and close the door behind them

Marie I hope the children won't misbehave when the photographer arrives, Miss Clay. They do seem to be asserting themselves more of late, and the excitement of having their photograph taken...

Miss Clay I'm sorry, Madame. I do try and see to it that they...

Marie (*smiling and sitting*) I wasn't criticizing you, Miss Clay. Indeed, the standard of your work has been quite excellent and I'm grateful to you.

Miss Clay That's very kind of you to say so, Madame la Marquise.

Act I   Scene 2

Marie It isn't kindness. It's the truth. Not only are you a good governess to the children you're also, when occasion requires it, a good companion to me.
Miss Clay I'm always honoured to be in your company, Madame.
Marie It's gratifying that you should think so. However, it is I who are indebted to you for your intelligent conversation and humour when my husband isn't here which, as you've noticed since you've been with us, is quite often. (*With a sudden thought*) I know, Miss Clay! We'll have a picture of *you* and the children taken together. The children would adore that.
Miss Clay Oh, no, Madame.
Marie Why ever not? You're an attractive young woman. Why should you be ashamed of having your photograph taken. You're not going to tell me that some respectable young man somewhere hasn't bothered to tell you how attractive you are?
Miss Clay (*embarrassed*) No, Madame. They have not.
Marie Men are blind. I've always said that. They strut about blinded by their own pride.

The telephone rings

I expect the photographer's arrived. Would you answer it?

Miss Clay goes to the telephone and answers it

Miss Clay Hello...Yes...This is Miss Clay the governess speaking...One moment. (*Turning to Marie*) It is Monsieur Paul, Madame. Would you like reception to send him up?
Marie Of course, Miss Clay. He can't take pictures of us downstairs can he?
Miss Clay No, Madame la Marquise.

Marie gets up and goes out on to the balcony

Would you ask him to come up please...Thank you. (*She replaces the receiver*)

On the balcony, Marie sighs deeply

Marie It's so hot. There's hardly anyone on the beach and the sea is as still as a millpond. (*Turning*) I hope the little photographer's sister isn't with him. (*She moves back into the room*) A dominating little creature I thought. Mind you, she's the one with the business brain. It's Monsieur Paul who's the artist. He's the one with the real talent judging by the pictures he has on display in his shop.
Miss Clay His sister seemed very self-sufficient, I thought.
Marie Serving behind a counter, I suppose one has to appear confident. Especially a woman. One has to overcome such indignities when one has to work for a living, I suppose.
Miss Clay (*hurt*) Indeed yes—Madame...

There is a knock on the door. Marie moves to the chaise-longue and arranges herself

Marie Would you let him in please, Miss Clay?

Miss Clay Yes, Madame.

Miss Clay goes to the door and opens it

> Outside holding a tripod camera and plates is Monsieur Paul. He is about twenty-two and small in stature. He is extremely handsome with a head of black curly hair and a fine, delicately chisled face. He comes into the room smiling and then we notice the limp and the black ugly club foot

Marie also notices the club foot, and her welcoming smile evaporates as she does so. She becomes acutely embarrassed, as does Miss Clay. Paul hobbles directly to Marie

Paul Madame la Marquise, I most humbly apologize for being late...
Marie Er—no matter. You—er—you've met Miss Clay of course...
Paul Ah—yes. How do you do, Miss Clay?
Miss Clay Monsieur Paul.
Paul I'd like to say Madame la Marquise how deeply honoured I am in being allowed to take photographs of you and your family...
Marie Not at all, Monsieur. My husband, unfortunately, has had to go to Paris so is unable to be with us this afternoon.
Paul Oh, I'm sorry. I hope that does not mean we shall have to cancel the afternoon's sitting...
Marie No. My husband would like some photographs of the children, and, of course, myself.
Paul I'm delighted, Madame. If you have no objection I'd like to set up my camera—er—here if that's convenient.
Marie As you wish.

Paul begins to prepare his camera

Paul I'd also like your permission to change the angle of the chaise-longue.
Marie (*indicating her approval*) Please...

Marie moves to the balcony and looks out over the sea. Paul smiles at Miss Clay as he places the camera in position. She smiles back.. He then moves to the chaise-longue and moves it so that it faces upstage to the camera

Marie (*turning*) It's very hot is it not, Monsieur Paul?
Paul It's always like this in August.
Marie Is it? Is it really? As hot as this? Always?
Paul Well—sometimes.
Marie I don't remember it being quite as oppressive as this last year. How do you survive?
Paul One gets used to it.

Marie moves into the room

Marie (*smiling at Miss Clay*) Er—Miss Clay?
Miss Clay Yes, Madame la Marquise?
Marie Monsieur Paul, is it all right if I bring in the children?
Paul But of course, Madame la Marquise. I'll be ready in a few seconds.
Marie Then if you'd be so kind, Miss Clay.

Act I   Scene 2

Miss Clay Yes, Madame.

Miss Clay exits to the children's room

Marie looks at Paul adjusting the camera and the positioning of the chaise-longue. He looks up at her and smiles. She returns the smile. There is a flash of mutual admiration between them

Marie I—er—I must apologize, Monsieur Paul.
Paul Apologize? Whatever for, Madame la Marquise?
Marie My behaviour—upon your arrival.
Paul I do not understand, Madame...
Marie I—er—must have seemed somewhat insensitive—when you came in. It's very polite of you, of course, to pretend you didn't notice our shortcomings...
Paul Madame, I believe you overstate the case. I am not offended.
Marie You are gracious, sir. You see, I was not aware of your—limp when you were in the shop. You were standing behind the counter at the time, you see, so...
Paul People look at first, Madame. But when they get used to it they think no more about it. Like me.
Marie Probably not. But someone so young—so—er... Anyway, my apologies.
Paul (*touched by her kindness*) You are very kind, Madame. (*Bowing*) And gracious. (*Rising*) And—very, very beautiful.

He moves towards her. Marie appears spellbound. He takes her hand and kisses it

The door opens, and Miss Clay and the children come in. Marie withdraws her hand and moves away like a child caught in the act of something dreadful

Marie Ah. There you are, children.
Paul Well, well, well. What beautiful pictures we shall take this afternoon.
Helene Are you the photographer?
Paul I am.
Helene Is this your camera?
Paul It is.
Helene Can I look through it?
Marie Monsieur Paul is a very busy man, Helene. He hasn't time to play with inquisitive children.
Celeste Can Miss Clay be in the picture?
Marie In a moment, Celeste. Now, Monsieur Paul. Where would you like us to sit?
Paul In the chaise, Madame la Marquise, if you'd be so kind. I imagined you sitting there—displaying that beautiful dress you're wearing, with the children standing behind you. It would be a portrait of such beauty.
Marie Very well. Now, children, round the back like Monsieur Paul says. I'll sit here. (*Leaning back and adjusting the dress*) Is this what you mean Monsieur Paul?
Paul (*standing back*) Now let me see. If—er—Celeste, is it?

Celeste Yes.

Paul If you could move in a little. That's better. (*Moving to Marie and kneeling before her, adjusting the hem of her dress*) Allow me, Madame.

As Paul is near her she becomes aroused and tense. Miss Clay notices the reaction. Marie glances at Miss Clay guiltily

(*Moving back*) That's better. Yes, I think that is excellent. Now I want you to remain perfectly still while I look at you through the lens of the camera—to see if the composition is good. Excuse me...

Monsieur Paul retreats behind the camera and under the black velvet cover. The girls start to giggle

Marie Celeste. Helene. What did Monsieur Paul say?

Celeste ⎫
Helene ⎭ To remain perfectly still, Mama. { *Speaking together* }

Marie Then kindly do so.

Celeste ⎫ Yes, Mama. ⎫ *Speaking*
Helene ⎭ Very well, Mama. ⎭ *together*

Paul (*coming out from behind the camera*) Just a slight adjustment, I think. (*He adjusts the lens and returns under the cloth*) Now. Please keep perfectly still. That's most important. I will count one to six...

Marie Very well, Monsieur Paul.

Paul Ready. Please don't move.

Paul removes the lens cover and the plate shield. Everyone is still as he counts one to six. He replaces the lens cover when he has finished, and the girls start to giggle

Marie Quiet, girls. Please.

Helene When can we see it? When can we see the picture?

Paul (*as he takes out the plate*) Not yet I'm afraid. It has to be developed. That takes a long time.

Helene Can I hide under that black thing, Monsieur Paul?

Celeste Me too—me too. Please, Mama, let me...

Helene I asked first, Mama...

Marie Helene! Celeste!

Paul I don't mind, Madame la Marquise, really. If they want to look through the lens I have no objections.

Marie However, I do, Monsieur Paul. (*To the girls*) I don't know what you're both thinking about. Your behaviour is appalling. Miss Clay!

Miss Clay I'm sorry, Madame la Marquise.

Marie Clearly they're over excited. No more photographs until they've calmed down and can behave themselves like normal, sensible children.

Helene (*tearfully*) Oh, Mama—I'm sorry...

Celeste ⎫ (*whining*) Honestly—we're sorry, Mama. We'll be
              good—we'll be good... ⎫ *speaking*
Helene ⎭ Please, Mama. Let us have some more pictures taken— ⎭ *together*
              please—please...

Celeste Oh, please Mama...

Act I Scene 2

Marie (*her anger showing*) Be quiet! Both of you! You're giving me a dreadful headache. Miss Clay, will you take them downstairs to the games room and let them release their energies there. I don't think I can manage anymore this afternoon.
Paul I'm sorry, Madame. I fear it was all my fault.
Marie It has nothing to do with you, Monsieur Paul. Children will be children. I have a headache developing, that's all....
Miss Clay Would you like me to get your pills, Madame?

The children cry and whine louder

Marie No. No. I'll be all right, Miss Clay. All I need is a little quiet.
Miss Clay (*going to the children and bundling them to the door*) Come along, children. We'll go downstairs. Now stop crying. You've upset your mother and Monsieur Paul... you've spoilt the whole afternoon.

The children cry louder as they reach the hall door

Marie Miss Clay.
Miss Clay Yes, Madame?
Marie While you're in the lounge would you ask them to send up some lemon tea.
Miss Clay Lemon tea for one. Very well, Madame.
Marie Er—for two, Miss Clay. You'll stay for a few moments longer won't you, Monsieur Paul? I'd hate to think I put you to so much trouble simply to take one photograph.
Paul Not at all, Madame. Another day, perhaps. I can always come back another day.
Marie That is true of course, but you'll join me now—in a cup of tea? Won't you?
Paul I'd be delighted. Thank you, Madame.
Marie (*to Miss Clay*) For two then, Miss Clay.
Miss Clay Very well, Madame. Come along, children.
Helene ⎫ (*as they leave*) We're sorry, Mama.   *speaking*
Celeste ⎭ We didn't mean to give you a headache, Mama.   *together*
Miss Clay Good afternoon, Monsieur Paul.
Paul Good afternoon, Miss Clay.

Miss Clay, Helene and Celeste exit

Marie leans back on the chaise-longue and gives a deep sigh of relief

Marie Children can be extremely tiring. Especially on a hot day like this.
Paul (*moving to get a new plate*) I imagine they can.

Pause. Marie watches Paul get the plate and put it into the camera. She watches his every graceful movement

Marie (*clearing her throat*) Er—does—does your foot hurt?
Paul Sometimes.
Marie Does it hurt now?
Paul Yes. The heat...
Marie And standing. All that standing can't be good for you.

Paul It doesn't help, that's true.
Marie You must be a very patient young man.
Paul Why do you say that?
Marie Because you must always be in pain.
Paul Madame la Marquise...
Marie Yes?
Paul May I ask a great favour of you?
Marie A favour? Why, yes, of course.
Paul May I be permitted to take a photograph of you—alone?
Marie Without the children, you mean?
Paul Yes. Like the way you're sitting now with the sunlight coming across the balcony behind you. It's turning your hair into gold and you look so beautiful...
Marie You're very kind, Monsieur Paul. Well, I suppose my husband would have no objection. Er—how then would you like me to pose?
Paul If you'd permit me.

He moves towards her. As he touches her she closes her eyes

If you would lean back a little...
Marie You'd like me to recline a little more? Is that what you want, Monsieur Paul?
Paul If you'd be so kind.

Marie moves lower into the chaise

Your headache, Madame. I forgot.
Marie (*gently*) So had I, Monsieur Paul.
Paul (*sitting beside her*) Now if—(*he gulps nervously*)—if you would slightly lift your head...
Marie Like this?
Paul Yes—look towards the camera, Madame. That's perfect. May I? (*Taking her hand*) Your arm should rest on your lap—so—more natural. Try and relax, Madame, you're tense. Your headache is making you tense.
Marie Please, Monsieur Paul, take your photograph.
Paul (*moving back to the camera*) Now, if you would keep quite still... (*He goes under the black velvet and looks through the lens*) That is perfection, Madame la Marquise. Perfection.

He comes out, replaces the plate shield and then removes the lens cover and silently counts to six. As he does so they look at each other wanting, needing. He replaces the lens cover

There. It's taken.
Marie (*slowly sitting up*) Will that be a good photograph do you think, Monsieur Paul?
Paul I'm sure of it, Madame la Marquise. You are extremely photogenic.
Marie I don't know whether that's a good thing to be or not. Doesn't the camera sometimes lie?
Paul The camera never lies, Madame. One more. May I take one more?
Marie You're becoming greedy, Monsieur Paul.

Act I Scene 2

Paul Forgive me.
Marie I don't know what my husband will say, but how would you like me to pose this time?
Paul Oh, thank you, Madame. Thank you. (*Moving towards her*) Standing perhaps. Behind the chaise-longue. Facing the balcony slightly but looking over your shoulder at the camera...
Marie Very well. (*Moving behind the chaise-longue and trying to pose*) It appears I need the abilities of a contortionist. Perhaps, Monsieur Paul, you would show me precisely how you'd like me to stand.
Paul If Madame wishes. (*Paul comes round the other side of the chaise-longue. He moves her into position. He is bolder this time, taking her chin in his hand and adjusting the angle of her head*)
Marie It's a very uncomfortable position...

Paul returns to the camera, takes out the previous plate and puts in a new one

Paul You look very beautiful—composed...
Marie I'm leaving the composition to you, Monsieur Paul. (*She laughs a little*) Please don't be much longer. It's doubtful whether my spinal cord can stand the strain.
Paul Please try and keep still a moment longer, Madame. I just have to adjust... (*He adjusts the lens, takes off the plate shield*)

Marie starts to giggle

Madame, please...
Marie I'm sorry.
Paul Now. Absolutely still.

He takes off the lens cover and counts to six. They look intently at each other as he does so. When it is over he replaces the lens cover

Marie Am I permitted to move now?
Paul Please, Madame la Marquise. I'm sorry if I've caused you any discomfort.
Marie As long as the results are worth it, Monsieur Paul. Well, I really think that will have to be all for today.
Paul Of course, Madame.
Marie Photography seems a very interesting profession.
Paul It's very skilled. Yes.
Marie To handle a camera needs skill, but so does the handling of your subjects surely?
Paul Yes. I suppose so...
Marie Well, you do both extremely well.
Paul Thank you.

Paul begins to pack up the camera after taking out the plate. Marie moves towards him slightly

Marie Is the shop yours, Monsieur Paul?
Paul Yes. And my sister's. It was left to us by my father.
Marie Your sister appears very competent in matters of business.

Paul Therese handles all the financial side of things.
Marie We're all good at different things. You are an artist, Monsieur Paul. I can tell. I like artistic young men. They have such understanding of— things...
Paul Understanding, Madame?
Marie Yes. They seem—well—they appear to understand women better.
Paul I must say I have never thought about it.
Marie Oh surely—you must have...

There is a pause—a long pause. As he packs the things away he is conscious that Marie is watching him. Suddenly there is a knock on the door

Come in.

The door opens. It is the Waiter with a tray of tea

(*Indicating the table by the chair*) On there, please.

The Waiter goes to the table indicated

Thank you.
Waiter Is that all, Madame la Marquise?
Marie Yes.

The Waiter leaves

Paul How long are you staying here, Madame?
Marie Another three weeks.
Paul Then there will be other opportunities.
Marie Opportunities, Monsieur Paul? For what?
Paul To photograph you, Madame.

Marie moves to the tea tray; she laughs gently

(*Moving to her; earnestly*) Please, Madame...You've such an exquisite face.
Marie You're embarrassing me with your flattery, young man.
Paul It's not flattery, Madame. (*Seriously*) I speak the truth. One cannot deny the truth.

She turns and looks at his face. It is deadly earnest. He looks away and then returns the chaise-longue back to its previous position

There. The room is back to normal again.
Marie (*moving towards him*) I have no objection to being photographed again. If you really want to.
Paul Want to? Oh, Madame, how can I thank you? What do I say in response to such kindness...(*He takes her hands and kisses them*)
Marie You're very demonstrative, Monsieur Paul.
Paul I'm sorry, Madame. I forgot...

They are now standing close to each other, looking into each other's eyes. There is a silence. Slowly Marie raises her hand and touches Paul's cheek. He takes the hand and holds it against his lips. Marie pulls away suddenly

Act I Scene 2

Marie Er—I think we should sit down.

He sits on the chaise-longue. Marie moves to the chair. She pours a cup of tea, then pours in the milk

    Monsieur... (*She clears her throat nervously*)
Paul Er—do you know the headland, Madame?
Marie Headland?
Paul It's at the southern end of the beach. You can see it from the balcony. Look, let me show you. Please...

He leads the way to the balcony. She follows, and stands behind him

    (*Looking off*) You see those cliffs at the end of the beach?
Marie Yes.
Paul Above that is the headland which sweeps round into another bay but it's very rocky there and there isn't a beach. Hardly anyone goes up there—except me.
Marie Oh? And what do you do there, Monsieur Paul? (*He turns and comes face to face with her*)
Paul I take pictures.
Marie Of what?
Paul Of nature. I take the most breathtaking views of sea and sky and sea birds. I take pictures of them in flight, free and restless, gliding in the wind. I take pictures of them swooping and fighting for food. I'm completely alone up there...

Marie moves back into the room

Marie Not strictly true, surely.
Paul I don't understand, Madame.
Marie You have all those birds for company. You have nature for company.
Paul (*nervously following her into the room*) I could take pictures of you up there—wonderful pictures, with the wind in your hair. You should be photographed in the open, where you're free...
Marie It all sounds very romantic. I'm tempted, Monsieur Paul. I can't promise, of course. Not just like that.
Paul Why not?
Marie Because—well—because I can't. It depends on so much.
Paul Can you imagine the exciting pictures I could take of you? Your husband would be pleased.
Marie No! My husband must never see pictures of me like that...
Paul (*staring at her*) Like what, Madame?
Marie What?
Paul What kind of pictures do you think I'm going to take, Madame?
Marie Well—informal pictures, I imagine. My husband is a very conservative man, Monsieur Paul. He would only approve of a formal pose...
Paul (*intensely*) But that's not you, Madame. Is it? That's not the real you.
Marie You're a persistent young man.
Paul Dare I hope that you're weakening, Madame? Just a little?
Marie (*suddenly*) You're impertinent, Monsieur Paul!

Paul (*realizing his position*) Please forgive me. Forgive me.

He moves towards her and kisses her hand. She moves as if to stroke his hair but refrains

Marie You're like a small boy—just like a small boy...
Paul (*looking up intensely into her eyes*) I am a man, Madame...
Marie (*after a moment*) Yes. Yes, of course. (*A long pause*) Very well, Monsieur Paul—I'll come.
Paul Thank you. (*He kisses her hand again, then looks up into her eyes*) Tomorrow, then.

The Lights fade to a BLACKOUT.

SCENE 3

The same. Early afternoon, two weeks later

Monsieur Paul's camera stands in the corner. It has not been used. His jacket lies on the chaise-longue. Otherwise the room is empty

As the Lights come up, the telephone rings. No-one answers it. It keeps ringing. Suddenly the hall door opens and Miss Clay enters. She closes the door, and is just about to pick up the receiver when the ringing stops. She turns to the children's room, when she notices the camera in the corner. Then she sees the jacket lying on the chaise. Her eyes move towards the door of Marie's bedroom. She then hurriedly tiptoes into the children's room. After a moment she returns, carrying a couple of buckets and spades. She leaves the door of the children's room open. She is just about to exit when the telephone rings again. She goes to answer it, but just as she is about to pick up the receiver she thinks better of it, and quietly exits. When the ringing stops, the door to Marie's room opens and Marie enters, wearing a beautiful negligé. She moves slowly down to the chaise. As she does so, Monsieur Paul enters, putting on his shirt

Marie That was probably Edouard telephoning from Paris. He calls nearly every day. (*She notices that the door to the children's room is open*) That door was closed when you arrived. Miss Clay must have returned. (*Moving to him*) I knew I heard someone moving about in here just now.
Paul Calm yourself, Marie.
Marie (*moving to the hall door and locking it*) She'll know. She'll have seen the camera, your coat...
Paul (*picking up his coat and putting it on*) Then there is little point in locking the door, is there?
Marie (*turning to him, anxiously*) Please hurry!
Paul When can I see you again?
Marie This is the second time this week.
Paul I want to see you every day, Marie. *Be* with you every day.
Marie It's impossible.
Paul Are you saying we *won't* meet again?
Marie Not here! (*Moving away*) It was a mistake, coming here.

Act I Scene 3

Paul There was always the chance that your servants would find out.
Marie You don't understand, do you?
Paul Miss Clay is loyal, isn't she?
Marie Of course. But there are other people in the hotel.
Paul Why should they know?
Marie They have eyes. They will draw their own conclusions. They will gossip.
Paul Where else can we go then? Except the headland?
Marie No! It's—er—it's too dangerous—too open...
Paul Then where, Marie?
Marie (*with a sudden inner panic*) I don't know. I just don't know. You must go.
Paul You're angry.
Marie (*going to him and touching his face*) Oh, no—my dear. Not with you. How could I be angry with you when you make me so happy?
Paul Then why concern yourself with what people think?
Marie You think it's all so simple.
Paul Loving someone is simple.
Marie For you maybe. Not for a woman in my position.
Paul I'm sorry. I do not understand that.
Marie Paul, listen to me. My husband is a most respected and admired businessman. He has friends everywhere. Some of them are very important. Our position in society will be destroyed if—if our association is discovered or even whispered about. Miss Clay must know of our meetings and—well—it gives me cause for concern.
Paul So Miss Clay knows. What of it?
Marie (*slightly embarrassed*) I'm concerned with what she might do with such knowledge. Do you not realize how vulnerable I have become?
Paul Look at me, Marie.

Marie does not respond

Look at me.

She looks at him

Is it not possible for love, true love, to transcend such things as social position and wealth? Isn't it more important that two people love each other as we do? (*No reply*) You don't love your husband.
Marie I have the children to think of.

Paul does not reply. Marie sees the disappointment on his face

My dear, I know you think I'm being selfish and ungrateful, especially when you've brought me such happiness, but you must try and understand that what is happening to me has never happened before. It's a new experience I'm living through and—well—I'm afraid. Not, you understand, of my love for you or your love for me, but what could happen if—well—if it all got out of hand.
Paul Out of hand? I don't think I...
Marie (*angrily*) You can't be as stupid as you pretend. (*She sighs nervously*) I'm sorry—really. I'm sorry I spoke like that but life isn't as black and white for me as it seems to be for you.

Paul You either love someone or you don't.
Marie *You* have only yourself to consider.
Paul That is not true. I am also thinking of you. I may have to work for my living, Marie, but I'm aware of what responsibilities befall a man when he loves someone as much as I love you.
Marie You're making things so difficult for me. I'm beginning to feel—hemmed in. Here we are in this room, hiding from the world, making love in the shadows behind locked doors, hiding from the servants—I didn't think it would be like this.
Paul (*after a pause*) I had better go. I'm sorry our love has brought you such—disappointment.
Marie Don't be angry with me. Please. I can't bear it when you're angry. I love you so much. These last few days have been the most wonderful, the most beautiful of my life...
Paul Then that is all that matters isn't it? If our love is impregnable. *We* are impregnable.

She looks at him momentarily. She sighs and smiles. He moves towards her and he takes her in his arms and kisses her passionately

Marie You overwhelm me.
Paul I will see you tomorrow and the day after...
Marie (*smiling helplessly*) I can't...
Paul Break away, Marie, break away and come with me.
Marie You haven't listened to a word.

He kisses her again, and she clings to him passionately. Then after a moment she breaks away, the awful consequences of her action beginning to grow again in her mind. She moves to the balcony

Paul What's the matter?
Marie (*almost in a whisper*) Go. Please go.
Paul When will I see you?
Marie The day after tomorrow.
Paul (*firmly*) Tomorrow.

She shakes her head

   Up on the headland.
Marie No.
Paul Tomorrow—midday...

She turns and looks at him

Marie You're bent on destroying me...
Paul (*strongly and passionately*) I'll never let you go, Marie. Not for one day. Not for one moment.

They look momentarily at each other, he with passion in his eyes, she with tears in hers. She can resist no longer. She rushes into his arms and holds him tightly. He smiles. He has won. There is a knock on the door. Suddenly Marie moves away

Act I Scene 3

Marie (*anxiously, her fingers to her lips*) Don't make a sound. Don't say a word.
Elise (*off*) Marie? Marie?
Marie Don't move, Paul. Please. She mustn't know.
Elise (*off*) Marie? I know you're there.
Paul (*whispering*) Sit down.
Marie No.
Paul Do as I say. Sit down.

Marie is reluctant at first, then she sits down on the chaise

Marie You must not let her in.

Knocking again. Paul gets his camera from the corner of the room and sets it down in front of the chaise

Elise (*off*) Marie, I know you're in there having your photograph taken. Why won't you let me in?

Paul goes to the door and unlocks it

Elise enters, and looks first at Paul and then at Marie

Marie I—er—I'm sorry I had to leave you waiting outside for a moment Elise.

Paul closes the door

This is Monsieur Paul. Monsieur Paul, this is an old friend of mine, Madame Brille.
Elise Monsieur Paul.
Paul Madame.
Elise I'm sorry if I arrived at an inconvenient moment.
Marie It was more inconvenient for Monsieur Paul than me. I'm only required to sit here—as you can see.
Elise With the door locked?
Marie Er—yes. I asked Monsieur Paul to lock the door because I didn't want the children rushing in here while he was working.
Elise (*smiling and indicating the closed plate box*) Well, I see you've finished. Everything neatly packed away.
Paul I was about to leave, Madame.
Elise Well, young man, if Madame la Marquise speaks highly of you I shall have to see if my husband will agree to have *my* photograph taken. I don't suppose I have such an eye catching—costume to wear as Madame la Marquise...
Marie (*embarrassed*) Er—thank you, Monsieur Paul. I—er—I hope these photographs will come out to your satisfaction this time.
Paul I hope so too, Madame. I regret I had to ask you to sit for me a second time.
Marie It seems, Elise, that the first selection of photographs I had taken didn't come out. Isn't that right, Monsieur Paul?
Paul (*to Elise*) It was a question of light, Madame.
Elise Light?

Paul It was my fault entirely. I didn't allow enough exposure time. As a result the pictures were unclear and dark. It simply did not do justice to Madame, who very kindly allowed me to return today and re-take the pictures I so carelessly spoiled.
Elise Well, if you have them ready before I leave I should be delighted to see your work, Monsieur Paul.
Marie If that's all, Monsieur Paul?
Paul Of course, Madame la Marquise.

Elise watches the looks between them carefully. As they talk, Monsieur Paul gathers his things together

Marie I—er—hope it won't be necessary for me to sit again.
Paul I hope so too, Madame. I will develop these right away. I will work all night if need be. If you happen to be walking in the village tomorrow morning I might be able...
Elise Such a rush!
Marie It's just that I'd like to have them finished and mounted before Edouard returns. He'll be anxious to see them.
Elise Yes. I'm sure.
Paul What time, Madame?
Marie Pardon?
Paul What time might it be convenient for you to call tomorrow?
Marie Er—I don't know. I'll have to think.
Paul Alternatively I could call here...
Marie (*sharply*) No. Er—no, I don't think that will be necessary. I'll call on you at the shop.
Paul Shall we say three o'clock, Madame?
Marie Three o'clock, Monsieur Paul.
Paul (*to Elise*) Good afternoon, Madame.
Elise Good afternoon, Monsieur Paul.
Paul (*to Marie*) Madame la Marquise.
Marie Monsieur Paul.

Paul exits

Elise (*smiling*) Well, well, well. So *that's* your little photographer.
Marie Not *my* little photographer, Elise. He is the *local* photographer.
Elise So handsome. So virile. You're right. He is attractive. But for his deformity...
Marie What is it you wanted, Elise?
Elise Had you forgotten, Marie, that we arranged to walk along the promenade this afternoon?
Marie Had we?
Elise Yes.
Marie Oh, Elise, how discourteous of me. I forgot.
Elise I had already come to that conclusion.
Marie The heat...
Elise The photographer...
Marie The *heat* is getting me down I fear. I'm forgetting many things lately.

Elise Really?

Marie glances at her

    Marie my dear, you can't fool me. (*Pause*) You're in love.
Marie Don't be ridiculous.
Elise It's written all over your face.
Marie He came to take my photograph, that's all.
Elise In your negligé? With the door locked?
Marie You don't need to read anything into that.
Elise I imagine your husband would if he had entered this room a moment ago. (*She laughs mischievously to herself*) I'm not condemning you. I'm pleased to see you acted upon my advice. He's immensely attractive. A great pity though—about the one blemish.
Marie Blemish?
Elise Him being a cripple. (*Laughing, as she moves to the balcony*) Tell me, Marie, wouldn't you like to stand on this balcony and shout above the sea, "I'm in love. I'm in love!" Just like that? So that everyone could hear? Hear all the way to Paris? (*Pause. She moves back to Marie and speaks seriously*) Instead, what is it we are forced to do? Be furtive—secretive. Hide behind a mask of true feelings, so that honour and position can remain intact...

The telephone rings. Marie answers it

Marie Hello...Yes, Miss Clay. What are you doing telephoning from the lounge?...(*Edgily*) Of course you may come up. The children should have changed for tea at least fifteen minutes ago...(*Glancing at Elise*) Yes. The photographer has gone.

Elise moves away smiling. Marie replaces the receiver

    (*Coldly*) I fear Miss Clay will have to go.
Elise Oh. Why?
Marie She's beginning to mistake kindness, my consideration, for weakness.
Elise That will never do, Marie. You mustn't be weak. A woman in your position must *never* be weak.

The Lights fade to a BLACKOUT.

SCENE 4

The same. Late afternoon, one week later

The stage is empty. Helene and Celeste are heard arguing in their bedroom

Helene (*off*) It's mine. I found it.
Celeste (*off*) No you didn't.
Helene (*off*) I found it.
Celeste (*off*) No you didn't.
Miss Clay (*off*) Celeste! Helene! Stop it at once. Arguing over a few shells.
Helene (*off*) It's a special shell, Miss Clay. And I found it.

Celeste (*off*) I found it first so you couldn't have found it before I did.
Miss Clay (*off*) If you don't stop this noise at once I shall have to tell your mama. Is that clear?
Celeste (*off*) Yes, Miss Clay.
Miss Clay (*off*) Helene?
Helene (*off*) Yes, Miss Clay.

The telephone rings

Miss Clay (*off*) As it is you're confined to this room for the rest of the day. (*Opening the door*) Don't let me hear another word.

Miss Clay comes in to answer the phone

(*On the phone*) Hello... No, I'm afraid the Marquise is out. It's Miss Clay, the governess, speaking... Paris? Oh, of course... I'll speak to the Marquis. Would you put him through, please... Thank you. (*There is a pause, then she speaks formally*) Monsieur le Marquis... No, sir, I'm afraid Madame is out... I don't know. She went out early this morning... Walking... Walking, sir... (*Becoming embarrassed*) Well, I don't know exactly when she'll be back. She didn't say... I suppose the last two weeks... After you left for Paris... Yes, walking every day... Yes, sir... Yes, sir... Shall I repeat that?... "Negotiations are nearly complete and you hope to motor down this week-end and then home."... Yes, sir. I'll tell Madame la Marquise... Yes, sir...

There is a knock at the door

Er... if she comes home in the next half hour?... Yes, I'll ask her to ring you... Good-bye, Monsieur le Marquis.

Miss Clay replaces the receiver and hurries to the door

Elise stands on the threshold. Her smile vanishes when she sees Miss Clay

Elise Oh.
Miss Clay Yes?
Elise Is Madame la Marquise in?
Miss Clay No. I'm afraid she isn't.
Elise But she'll be in shortly, will she not?
Miss Clay Yes. I'm expecting her any minute.
Elise (*sweeping in*) Well, I'm sure she won't mind me waiting...
Miss Clay I'm sorry, Madame. May I enquire...
Elise I'm an old friend. I take it you're Miss Clay, the governess?
Miss Clay (*closing the door*) That's right. I'm sorry but I don't think... (*Suddenly realizing*) Oh—you must be Madame Brille.
Elise That's correct. (*She sits on the chaise-longue*)
Miss Clay I do apologize. I recognize you now. You've been keeping Madame la Marquise company these last two weeks.
Elise Yes, when she's been available. She seems to have allowed the observation of nature to take up a considerable amount of her time.
Miss Clay Nature? I don't think I understand, Madame.

Act I Scene 4

Elise Walking, Miss Clay. I've never seen anyone take up an outdoor activity with such devotion so quickly.
Miss Clay Madame la Marquise has always been an active person...
Elise Has she? Has she really? (*Pause*) Well, Miss Clay. How do you like being a governess in such a distinguished household?
Miss Clay I am well satisfied, Madame.
Elise No possibility of children of your own, eh? An attractive young woman like you?
Miss Clay Not for the moment, Madame. Well, if you'll excuse me I ought to see to the children.
Elise Where are they?
Miss Clay In the bedroom.
Elise Then they're quite safe, aren't they? You mustn't fuss too much over children, otherwise they'll lead you a dance and your life will never be your own. Tell me, Miss Clay. Will Madame la Marquise be long?
Miss Clay I do not know.
Elise Then you can keep me company while I wait. Come and sit down—next to me. (*Patting the space next to her*) I want to hear what's been going on during the last two weeks.
Miss Clay Going on, Madame? I don't understand.
Elise (*smiling*) Come, Miss Clay. There's no need to be afraid. I've known your employer since we were at school together.
Miss Clay Yes I'm sure, but...
Elise So you will appreciate that I'm an old and well trusted friend.

Miss Clay reaches the chaise-longue

Come on. Sit down. I won't bite.

Miss Clay sits

Yes. Madame la Marquise and I know all there is to know about each other. (*She looks at Miss Clay's face and sighs*) I take it you do smile—occasionally, Miss Clay?
Miss Clay Yes.
Elise On fine weather days, perhaps?
Miss Clay I'm sure Madame la Marquise will be here soon. If you wish to wait you are, of course, free to do so. As for myself I have to carry on with my duties. (*She stands*)
Elise Your attitude is no doubt very correct, Miss Clay, but it is also being distinctly unhelpful to me. Perhaps that is your intention?
Miss Clay Madame la Marquise is out walking, Madame.
Elise I know she's out walking. Where?
Miss Clay I don't know.
Elise Sit down, Miss Clay.

Miss Clay sits

Madame la Marquise is out walking—in this heat?
Miss Clay She doesn't feel the heat as much as some.

There is a pause, then Elise smiles

Elise You're very loyal and your loyalty is to be admired. It's just that Madame la Marquise invited me to have tea with her at four o'clock. It's now ten past and no-one seems to know where she is. She also invited me to have tea with her yesterday asking me to meet her in the lounge downstairs. Neither appointment has she kept. I invited Madame la Marquise to have morning coffee with me a week ago on the terrace. Once again she didn't arrive. I just wondered, that's all...
Miss Clay "Wondered", Madame?
Elise What other pressing engagements have distracted Madame from enjoying our renewed acquaintance? Three times we have arranged to meet. Three times the meeting has proved elusive.
Miss Clay Madame la Marquise has been out walking a great deal lately.
Elise I've already gathered that, Miss Clay. However, I still find it difficult to believe Madame la Marquise has suddenly found walking such an attractive occupation. Madame has never walked anywhere in her life—and enjoyed it!
Miss Clay I've only been in her employ two years, Madame...
Elise Then you've had adequate opportunity to know I am right.
Miss Clay If you'll excuse me for saying so, Madame Brille. I think it unkind of you to take advantage of your position...
Elise I only came to make enquiries, Miss Clay. To see whether Madame la Marquise has taken my advice.
Miss Clay Advice?

Elise stands suddenly

Elise Er—just a small matter we discussed. One thing more, Miss Clay. Is your mistress doing all this walking alone?
Miss Clay I—have no idea...
Elise Miss Clay, you can rely on me. I won't breathe a word to anyone about this conversation.
Miss Clay We've had no conversation, Madame.
Elise You're being deliberately obtuse!
Miss Clay (*standing*) If you'll excuse me.
Elise Sit down, Miss Clay!

Miss Clay sits. There is a pause

(*Glancing at Miss Clay*) I think it's the little photographer she mentioned.
Miss Clay We did have some photographs taken.
Elise Of Madame and the children. Yes, I know. I told you, Miss Clay, Madame la Marquise and I don't have secrets from one another.
Miss Clay In that case, Madame Brille, you can wait a little longer for Madame la Marquise to return. Then you can learn what you want to know directly from her own lips.

Miss Clay gets up and exits into the children's bedroom

Elise (*to herself, angrily*) Why, you...!!

Elise glances at her watch, then wanders on to the balcony and looks out. As she does so there is a knock on the door. She turns and calls

Act I   Scene 4

Come in!

The door opens and the Waiter comes in with a trolley containing a teapot, cakes, etc.

Waiter   Madame la Marquise ordered tea, Madame.
Elise (*testily*)   How nice. Perhaps *you'll* join me.

Miss Clay enters to see who has arrived

As you can see, Miss Clay, tea has arrived. For two.
Miss Clay   So I see.

Miss Clay exits

Elise (*to the Waiter*)   Put it over there, will you, please?

The Waiter moves the trolley where indicated

Waiter   Would you like me to set it out, Madame?

The main door opens and Marie, unsmiling, tense, ashen, hurries in. She glances at Elise, then goes quickly into her room. There is desperation in her movements

Elise (*sensing something is very wrong*)   Marie?

The bedroom door shuts. The Waiter stares awkwardly

(*To the Waiter*)   Er—you can go. (*Loudly*) Hurry!

The Waiter goes

Elise at once hurries to the bedroom door and tries to open it. It is locked

(*Calling*)   Marie! Open the door! Please!

The children's door opens, and Miss Clay enters

Miss Clay   Is anything the matter?
Elise (*embarrassed*)   Er—no...
Miss Clay   Has Madame la Marquise returned?
Elise   Yes. She's—er—just gone into the bedroom for a handkerchief. Then we're going to have tea.
Miss Clay   Then would you be kind enough, Madame Brille, to tell Madame la Marquise that I have taken the children downstairs for their tea.
Elise   Certainly, Miss Clay.
Miss Clay   And that Monsieur le Marquis phoned from Paris a few moments ago. I think he'd like to speak to her.
Elise   I will tell Madame la Marquise.
Miss Clay   Thank you.

Miss Clay goes out

Elise goes to the bedroom door and listens

Elise   Marie, please come out. (*Pause*) Whatever it is—we can talk about it. Perhaps I can help...

Marie (*off*) Are you alone?
Elise Yes.

As the key in the lock turns, Elise moves away from the door

  Marie comes out and moves to the chaise-longue

Elise is distressed at Marie's appearance, which is one of great foreboding. She goes to her

  (*Almost whispering*) Marie? In God's name. What has happened?
Marie (*tensely*) You're a good friend, Elise. Say you're a good friend.
Elise (*taking her hands*) You know I am.
Marie I'm shaking. You feel me shaking?
Elise Please, Marie. Tell me.
Marie (*sitting on the chaise-longue*) I've—I've killed the photographer.

Elise cannot believe what she hears

Elise What?
Marie (*through tears*) I killed him. A young, crippled boy. He's out there now. In the sea. And I killed him, Elise—because he loved me too much...
Elise Marie, what are you saying?
Marie (*hysterically*) Don't you understand? I killed him—I killed him—I killed him!
Elise (*shaking her*) *Stop it!* Control yourself.
Marie (*helplessly*) Please help me—please...

Elise holds Marie's head against her breast. She sobs quietly while Elise strokes Marie's hair like a child. After a moment the crying subsides a little

Elise There can be no mistake?

Marie shakes her head

  That he's dead, I mean.

Marie shakes her head

  You say you—murdered...?
Marie Yes—yes...
Elise How?
Marie We were on the clifftop. There was an argument. His anger turned into a rage. I thought he was going to hit me. We fought like animals—like animals, Elise.... Oh God, it was terrible, dreadful, humiliating. I didn't think I was capable of such violence... (*She dabs her eyes, the tears choking her again. Pause*) What am I to do, Elise? Please tell me. What's the right thing to do...?
Elise Go to the police. That would be the right thing to do.
Marie (*with a sudden horrifying thought*) No! No, that's impossible. I'm not thinking of myself. I've done a terrible wrong and I want to die...
Elise You mustn't talk of dying, Marie...
Marie It's the shame, the ruin that would befall Edouard and the children ... (*Suddenly*) The children, Elise. What would become of my children?

Act I Scene 4

Elise Marie! Please! You're making it impossible to think. (*Pause*) There's no question of you going to the police. I'm involved now, or hadn't that occurred to you? I too have a certain position...
Marie How are you involved?
Elise I'm partly to blame for this. I advised you to have an affair, to take a lover.
Marie (*bitterly*) Oh, God! If Edouard had been here this wouldn't have happened...

Suddenly the telephone rings. Marie is startled

I can't speak to anyone. I can't see anyone. Don't answer it, Elise.
Elise We have to. You must have been seen coming into the hotel...
Marie It's probably Edouard calling from Paris.
Elise No. Miss Clay told me he phoned a few moments ago before I arrived. He wants you to call back.
Marie Oh my God—I can't speak to Edouard now. Not now...
Elise Marie! Please try and keep calm so that we can think.
Marie (*putting her hands to her ears*) If only that phone would stop.

After a moment the telephone stops. Silence. Elise sighs and sits beside Marie

(*desperately*) Oh, Elise—what am I to do?
Elise If I'm to help you, Marie, you must tell me everything. How did it happen?
Marie We've been meeting nearly every day since he first took photographs of the children and myself.
Elise Here, in the hotel?
Marie No. On the headland. Here on two occasions only.
Elise You went to bed together?
Marie Yes.
Elise And the headland—you made love there too?
Marie (*tensely*) Yes—yes—we made love there too. (*In desperation*) Oh, God! He wanted me to go there yesterday...
Elise And did you?
Marie I couldn't. I—er—wouldn't. It seemed to upset him. I thought I should spend a day with the children. Or at least be here when Edouard phoned. He wouldn't listen. We argued, and then he said he loved me so much that he was going to follow me back to Paris.
Elise What?
Marie I told him that was impossible. But he said he was not going to let me out of his sight—ever. He'd come to Paris, buy a small apartment from the money he'd make selling his shop and we'd be able to meet as often as we liked. Well, Elise, you can see his love for me had become an obsession. I had to do something. I insisted that when I returned to Paris he was to forget me. He accused me of deceit, of playing with his emotions. Suddenly, he changed, from a sweet, tender boy into a brute. He gripped my arms until his nails drew blood. He shouted at me and as I looked into his eyes they were full of hate. He threatened to tell Edouard. I struggled to get free of him and then—I noticed we were close to the edge of the cliff and

I realized—in a flash—he could be out of my life forever—that no longer would he be a danger—so...(*She stops. Pause*)
Elise You pushed—him?

Marie nods

(*With a deep sigh*) Dear God....
Marie I want to die, Elise. To have this on my conscience...(*She starts to cry*)
Elise Listen, Marie!

Marie wipes the tears from her eyes

Did anyone see the two of you up there?
Marie No. To my knowledge no-one knew of our regular meetings there.
Elise Did his sister know of the affair?
Marie I don't think so.
Elise Aren't you sure?
Marie We never discussed his sister. I constantly stressed how important it was that we keep our relationship secret. As far as I know he spoke to no-one of it.
Elise If, as you say, no-one knows of your affair, that it really has been a closely guarded secret...
Marie I swear it has.
Elise Then there is only one course open to you.
Marie What?
Elise You do precisely nothing.
Marie Nothing? But he's dead. They'll find his body. It'll be washed up somewhere...
Elise He was a photographer. It would be natural for a photographer to go up there on the headland with its spectacular views. The sister will report her brother's disappearance and the police will put two and two together. That there was an accident.
Marie (*seeing the possibilities of this*) An accident?
Elise Yes.
Marie (*liking the thought*) An accident. He slipped while photographing the birds...
Elise More important, Marie. That he was alone when he slipped. The ground must be uneven, stony. For a man with his deformity the dangers are obvious. I'm sure that is what the police will think.
Marie But if they don't? What is the alternative, Elise, if they don't believe it was an accident?
Elise Suicide. (*Pause*) Because of his love for you. Monsieur Paul killed himself while the balance of his mind was disturbed.
Marie That would involve me—openly.
Elise Yes. But only as an innocent party. You were unaware of his love for you. After all a Marquise having anything to do with an insignificant little photographer, and a cripple at that, is too preposterous to contemplate. No. Monsieur Paul killed himself because he knew that he could never have his love returned. That as far as he was concerned you were a prize beyond his reach. He was depressed at the thought and so killed himself.

Act I Scene 4

Marie (*brightening significantly; taking on a more aristocratic pose*) It sounds plausible—very plausible. An accident...
Elise (*edged very slightly with sarcasm*) Plausible enough to make you want to go on living?

Marie does not reply, too wrapped up in the lie Elise has planted in her mind

Wipe your eyes, Marie. Try and forget Monsieur Paul. Forget how foolish you've been.
Marie (*tonelessly*) It was an accident—of course...
Elise Keep saying it to yourself. Say it over and over again while you sit here quietly, relaxing...
Marie An accident...
Elise I believe you to be safe.
Marie An accident...
Elise Behave like a Marquise, Marie. You're safe. Believe me. You're perfectly safe.

CURTAIN

ACT II

Scene 1

The same. Three days later

As the Curtain *rises, Marie is sitting on the chaise-longue nervously reading a newspaper, devouring every word. Elise stands on the balcony looking at the activity on the beach. After a minute she glances over her shoulder at Marie and moves back into the room towards her*

Marie (*lowering the paper*) Pursuing enquiries... The police are pursuing enquiries. That's what it says.
Elise Naturally.
Marie Enquiries that could lead to me.
Elise It's possible. Yes. But if you were telling the truth about the secrecy with which you conducted the affair there is no reason why you should be involved.

The hall door opens urgently. Miss Clay enters with the newspaper

Miss Clay Madame la Marquise... (*Seeing the paper*) Oh—you've seen the newspaper...
Marie Er—yes—Madame Brille brought it to me. (*Trying to be composed*) It is most tragic.
Miss Clay Yes, Madame, so young, too...
Marie I shall send a note of condolence to his sister immediately.
Miss Clay I gather she will be totally alone in the world.
Marie Is that so?
Miss Clay So it says in the newspaper report, Madame.
Marie Are there no relatives?
Miss Clay None that can take care of her.
Marie A woman alone. It will be very hard.
Miss Clay I was wondering, Madame...
Marie Yes, Miss Clay?
Miss Clay Well—whether we should send flowers to the funeral. I mean, I would be willing to contribute a little...
Marie Yes. A good idea.
Elise Do you think that wise, Marie?

Miss Clay looks at Elise, who manages a fleeting smile

Marie Er—let me think a moment. Perhaps not. We don't want to become too involved in what is, after all, merely an accident... (*Seeing the look on Miss Clay's face*) I have to remember my position, Miss Clay.
Miss Clay I wouldn't have mentioned it of course, Madame, but, well—he did seem rather fond of you—the children as well, of course.

Act II Scene 1   37

Elise moves away, hoping Marie will keep her head

Marie Did he?
Miss Clay Oh, yes, Madame.
Marie (*trying to rise above the suggestion*) I hadn't noticed. He took some photographs of us, that's all. He was only a photographer, Miss Clay. I think—well—I think it would be wrong—perhaps wrong is too strong a word—I think it would be imprudent to send flowers to the funeral. I mean it's not as if he was a close friend of the family or even a relative. Why, we hardly knew the young man. I think such action—however kind—could be misconstrued.
Miss Clay You're right, Madame, of course. I should not have mentioned it.
Marie Not at all, Miss Clay. It was a very kind and humane thought. But I think we shouldn't, for appearance's sake. That's all. But I will send a note. I'll do it right away. This very moment.
Miss Clay I'll return to the beach, Madame. I've left the children long enough.
Marie Thank you, Miss Clay.

Miss Clay goes to hall door and exits

I'd forgotten about her. His sister.
Elise (*moving to the chaise*) What about her?
Marie He might have spoken to her about me.
Elise It largely depends what he said doesn't it? A man doesn't usually discuss details of his love affairs with his own sister does he?
Marie I shouldn't have thought so. No. (*She sighs heavily*) I wish I'd never come to this place. I hate it. I hate everything about it. The beach. That awful oppressive village with its cobblestones and disgusting little houses. And I hate him. Above all I hate the little photographer. Forced to wait here. Hiding. Afraid of being found out. A common little photographer with a club foot. Why, Elise? Why did I fall for such a creature?

There is a pause. Marie quietly sobs

Elise You've reached the restlessness of middle age. You have the urge to do things before it's too late. A love affair with—this peasant spelt uncertainty, danger even. It is this that appealed to you. Excited you, even. It was inevitable.

Marie wipes her tears away

Marie You make me feel ashamed.
Elise Why? Because you fell in love with another man?
Marie Unclean, then.
Elise Because you yearned for sex? Because the little photographer made you feel like a woman and you, in all probability, made him feel like a man. What's so wrong in that?
Marie What's wrong, Elise, is that I'm married—with two children.
Elise Oh, Marie. I know it's not my place to say this, but how often do you see your children? How often have you played with them since you've been

here on holiday? How many times have you sat with them on the beach? Your children love their governess more than they love you.

Marie (*angrily*) That's not true!

Elise You aren't involved in a marriage, Marie. You're simply living in the same house. What you love is the status marriage to Monsieur le Marquis has given you. And that's what you live in dread of losing.

Marie I sit here listening to you criticize me and my marriage when from what you've told me, yours isn't above reproach.

Elise I have a lover and a husband. True. But at least they are based on genuine relationships. I love my husband as a dutiful wife should. I'm there when he needs me. I run his house efficiently and I play hostess to his guests when it is required of me. As for Gerard, I love him for the way he satisfies my physical needs as a woman. And I enjoy the way I satisfy his needs as a man. But your squalid little affair with this young photographer was no more than a bit of holiday fun. You relished the thought of living and behaving like a peasant for a week or two—something that could only be enjoyed when you have comfort and security to return to.

Marie How dare you talk to me like that!

Elise And how dare you try and blame me for what has happened. I share some guilt in this I don't deny it. But remember. I didn't push that poor cripple off the cliff.

Marie now takes a pose. She seems to grow in stature. She becomes a real Marquise. She stands

Marie You listen to me, Elise. There was nothing between this wretch and myself. He came here and took some photographs. And, as a result of my generous patronage, he took advantage of me. He made my life miserable. If Edouard had been here I would have confided in him and no doubt he would have taken appropriate action. As it was it was left to me to deal with the situation. I went up to the cliffs one day. Alone. He followed me. He confronted me saying he was going to come to Paris. I explained the impracticability of it. He attacked me and in attempting to defend myself he slipped on the cliff edge and fell. It was an accident. Unfortunate, yes. But it *was* an accident. That's all I need to say on this matter should it ever get to the courts. And it's all I shall say now.

Marie moves to the bedroom door and then goes in

Elise is left alone. She looks after Marie astounded at her belief in what she has just said. She thinks for a moment: should she go to the door or not? She gets up, uncertain what to do. Then the telephone rings. She waits momentarily for Marie to come out and answer it. Marie does not. Elise answers it instead

Elise Hello?...No. Madame la Marquise is lying down. Yes...Who?... Who did you say is downstairs?...Er—no. No. Don't send her away. I'm sure Madame la Marquise would wish to see her. Yes. Ask her to come up, will you? Thank you.

Elise replaces the receiver, walks to the bedroom door and knocks. No reply

Marie...(*No reply*) Marie...

Act II Scene 1   39

Marie (*off*) Go away, Elise. I don't wish to see or speak to you again.
Elise Very well. I hope you don't have further need of me. (*Pause*) Someone is on their way up to see you. (*She waits. There is no reply*) Marie...?

Seeing nothing is going to be achieved, Elise leaves. After a moment the bedroom door opens and Marie comes out. She has been crying, and wipes the tears from her cheeks. She sits on the chaise-longue and after a moment she looks up to heaven

Marie (*softly, very sadly, almost like a prayer*) When I die I shall be punished. I don't fool myself. I am guilty of taking life. When I die, God will accuse me. Until then, I will be a good wife to Edouard and a good mother to Celeste and Helene. I will try to be a good woman from now on. I will try and atone for what I've done by being kinder to everyone, to relatives and servants...

Suddenly the hall door bursts open and Celeste and Helene rush in

The entrance frightens Marie, who is taken aback by the onslaught of her children

Celeste Mama—Mama....
Marie W–What in Heaven's name!
Helene Can we go on a boat?
Celeste Miss Clay's going to ask you...
Marie Please, children—bursting in on me like that...
Celeste Can we please? We'll be good. We promise. Can we please?
Marie Can you what?

Miss Clay comes in, closing the door

Miss Clay I'm sorry, Madame. They wouldn't wait.
Marie What is all this excitement?
Celeste Ask Mama, please, Miss Clay.
Helene Go on, Miss Clay.
Marie Ask me what?
Celeste We've been invited on to a boat.
Helene A big white boat.
Marie What is all this about, Miss Clay?
Miss Clay I'm sorry, Madame. It was all my fault really.
Marie Children, be quiet, please. Sit down quietly and you can tell me all about it. Come on. Sit by me.

Marie gathers the children around her on the chaise-longue. Her sudden motherly approach does not go unnoticed by Miss Clay

That's better. You're very hot, Celeste. You mustn't exert yourself so. You'll get heatstroke. Now, Miss Clay, tell me what's happened.
Miss Clay Well, Madame, I met this gentleman on the beach...
Marie Gentleman? What gentleman?
Miss Clay An elderly widower who turns out to be a Lord.
Marie A Lord? From England?
Miss Clay Yes, Madame.

Marie Well, Miss Clay, you have come up in the world. Talking to a Lord...
Miss Clay Oh no, Madame. You misunderstand. He spoke to me first.
Marie So I should think. Please go on.
Miss Clay Well, he seemed taken with the children, and it seems his wife died recently and he has two boys and a girl aboard his yacht, *The Adventurer*. It's anchored just beyond the headland. Well, his children and Celeste and Helene were getting on so well together that he invited them, and myself, of course, on board for tea this afternoon.
Marie Really?
Celeste Can we go, Mama?
Helene Please. It's a lovely boat.
Miss Clay It would be quite safe, Madame.
Marie But a complete stranger.
Miss Clay A Lord, Madame.
Marie Byron was a Lord, Miss Clay.
Miss Clay Yes, Madame.
Celeste Oh, please...
Helene Please, Mama...
Marie (*putting her arms around her children*) You want to go, don't you, my darlings?
Celeste Oh, yes. It's a beautiful boat. You should be able to see it from here, Mama...
Marie I've seen yachts before...
Celeste Not like this. Come on...
Helene Come on...

Helene and Celeste drag Marie from the chaise-longue to the balcony. The children point out the distant yacht. They talk quietly among themselves with Marie taking an uncommon interest in their conversation. Miss Clay looks at them smiling until she hears a gentle tapping on the door. Marie and the children continue to talk. Miss Clay moves to the door and opens it

> Standing outside is a young woman dressed entirely in black. It is Therese, Monsieur Paul's sister, aged about twenty-one: yet she looks older, and her sombre, stark appearance sends a shiver down Miss Clay's spine. During the scene that follows she acts with dignity, but intent on her true purpose

Miss Clay Mademoiselle Paul?
Therese I'd like to see Madame la Marquise please.
Miss Clay (*glancing over her shoulder*) I don't think...
Therese (*pointedly*) I'd like to see her. It's important.

Therese hobbles into the room, and Miss Clay is horrified to see that she too limps like her brother, though her club foot is hidden by her long dress. Suddenly, as Miss Clay closes the door, the children give a whoop of delight as Marie agrees that they can go on the yacht. They turn to run back to Miss Clay

Helene } We can go. We can go. { *Speaking*
           } We can go, Miss Clay. Mama says we can go. { *together*

They stop short as they see Therese. Marie also turns and she too now sees the

Act II Scene 1   41

figure in black. Her hand goes to her chest as the sight startles her. Then she realizes who she is. There is an awkward silence

Miss Clay Mademoiselle Paul insisted on seeing you, Madame la Marquise.
Marie (*trying to remain calm*) Oh, yes. Of course. Er—Miss Clay—it is in order for the children to go on the yacht providing you are satisfied with the arrangements.
Miss Clay Thank you, Madame.
Marie Er—I suggest you take the children and make them change for luncheon. It's almost noon.
Miss Clay Right away, Madame. Come along, children.
Celeste Thank you, Mama. (*To Therese*) We're going on a yacht.
Helene (*to Therese*) This afternoon. For tea...
Miss Clay Children...

Helene and Celeste follow Miss Clay into their bedroom

There is a long pause before Marie speaks

Marie Er—won't you sit down, Mademoiselle?
Therese Thank you, Madame.

Therese hobbles to the chair. Marie notices and she trembles

Marie I—er—I was not told you were here, Mademoiselle...
Therese I'm sorry, Madame. The receptionist did speak to someone in this room, however, and was informed that it would be in order to come up.
Marie I see. Still, no-one told me of your arrival.
Therese Well, I don't know who it was he spoke to, but he was told...
Marie Yes, I'm sure he was, Mademoiselle Paul. I don't doubt your word.

Marie moves to the chaise-longue and sits down

(*Clearing her throat*) I—er—I'm sorry about the children. They're rather excited today.
Therese Are they?
Marie They've been invited onto a yacht this afternoon. Belongs to a member of the British aristocracy. I couldn't refuse.
Therese No, of course not.
Marie I—er—I was going to write you a note, Mademoiselle. A letter of condolence...
Therese That's very thoughtful of Madame.
Marie But seeing that you're here—I can express myself to you directly.
Therese You saw the newspaper report, then?
Marie Yes. It was brought to my attention. Naturally, I wish to extend to you my deepest sympathy on your great loss, Mademoiselle.
Therese Thank you.
Marie If I can be of any possible help please do not hesitate to ask. Er—would you like some tea?
Therese No, thank you.
Marie It would only take a minute.
Therese No, thank you, Madame.

Marie Then, if you'll allow me, I'll arrange for transport to take you home. You shouldn't walk in all this heat with...
Therese With what, Madame. My deformity? My club foot?
Marie (*embarrassed*) Well, it is a consideration...
Therese My brother and I managed. (*She almost whispers*) Until you came along. I will walk home, Madame.
Marie As you wish. Excuse me a moment will you?

Marie gets up and hurries to her bedroom

Therese remains quite still, looking about at the room. Then she brings out an envelope from under her coat

Marie returns

Mademoiselle, I realize only too well that the death of your brother is a dreadful blow, and because of that you will find it very difficult to see the future clearly. At moments like this, when one's grief is all consuming, it is difficult to see any future at all. But I want you to take heart, Mademoiselle Paul. For life has to continue. You will have to go on and you will, I assure you, find the strength to carry on your life. Do you understand?

Therese merely looks at Marie. It causes Marie dreadful uneasiness

I did not know your brother well, of course, but I'm sure he was hardworking, offering you protection and security. There is very little I can do in such circumstances, but I hope that this small gift may help you to overcome your immediate needs.

Marie hands Therese a five hundred franc note. Therese looks at it as Marie presses it into her hand

Of course, I will send flowers to the funeral if you will let me know where it is taking place. I'm leaving for Paris tomorrow morning, otherwise I might have attended in person...
Therese Madame...
Marie Yes?
Therese (*through tears*) Madame la Marquise...
Marie Please, my dear. I know five hundred francs is very little, but at least it will cover the funeral expenses.

Therese wipes the tears from her face as she regains her composure. She looks straight at Marie

I—I wish I could do more...
Therese Madame la Marquise...
Marie Yes.
Therese Why do you think I came here this morning?
Marie I—I don't understand...
Therese You haven't asked me why I came to see you. What I'm doing here now? (*Crumpling the note*) You think I came here for this?
Marie Not at all, Mademoiselle Paul.
Therese Then why do you think I'm here?

Act II Scene 1   43

Marie (*an ominous feeling overtaking her*) I don't know, Mademoiselle.
Therese Madame. My brother was all I had in the world. He was good to me.
Marie I'm sure he was. Haven't I just said so...
Therese So what am I to do now? How am I to live?
Marie Relatives, perhaps...
Therese What relatives I have are poor folk. Very poor, Madame. I cannot expect them to support me. Nor can I keep on the shop alone without my brother. I haven't the strength. My health has always been against me. My brother you see, was strong. Very strong.
Marie I'm sorry—about your health...
Therese (*looking straight at Marie*) So, Madame—perhaps you would take a look at these. (*She hands Marie the envelope*)
Marie What is this?
Therese Photographs, Madame.
Marie (*opening the envelope*) Oh, the portraits of the children and... (*Seeing the photographs: fearfully*) What do these mean?
Therese Your photographs, Madame. Not the ones you expected, perhaps.

Marie tears them to pieces

    I have others.
Marie (*whispers*) Oh, my God.
Therese Photographically speaking, they were some of the best that Paul ever took. You see what they are don't you, Madame? You. Lying in the bracken, laughing, smiling, your dress open...
Marie I didn't know he was actually photographing me. I thought—I thought he was playing about—pretending—teasing...
Therese These pictures of course reveal a very different woman from the one who sits in this room. From the woman perhaps her husband knows so well.

Pause

Marie What do you want me to do?
Therese I have lost my dear brother, Madame.
Marie I'm aware of that.
Therese My supporter, my reason for being alive. Madame la Marquise has had an enjoyable holiday and is to return home tomorrow. I take it that Madame would not desire her husband and family to see those photographs.
Marie I don't even wish to see them myself.
Therese In which case twenty thousand francs is really very little return for a holiday that Madame has so much enjoyed.
Marie I see. What I have given you is all I have.
Therese It will do to start.
Marie I see...
Therese Do you, Madame?
Marie Yes. I have a little more money downstairs in the safe deposit box...
Therese I thought you might.
Marie A few thousand.

Therese Then you can arrange for that to be brought upstairs sometime. I'll call in tomorrow morning. Before you leave for Paris.
Marie No. If you can come back this afternoon I can arrange...
Therese I cannot come back this afternoon, Madame. I will visit you tomorrow morning before you leave. And I think it would be more satisfactory for both of us if we came to a more permanent arrangement. Now my brother has gone the future is uncertain. Besides, I might not wish to live in a neighbourhood that holds such sad memories. Then there are other questions that need answering. For instance, how my brother met his death. The afternoon before he disappeared he went out to the headland and came back very distressed. I knew something had upset him but I did not ask him what. Perhaps he had hoped to meet a friend and that friend had not appeared. Eh, Madame? The next day he went again, and that night he did not return. The police were informed, and then, three days later, his body was found. I have said nothing of possible suicide to the police, but have accepted it as they have done, as accidental. But then again, my brother was a very sensitive person, Madame la Marquise. Unhappy, deeply hurt, he would be capable of—anything. If I make myself wretched thinking over these things, I might go to the police, I might suggest that Paul did away with himself after an unhappy love affair. I might even give them permission to search his effects—the photographs in his dark room. Do you understand, Madame?
Marie Perfectly, Mademoiselle.
Therese I'm glad. (*She slowly gets up and goes to the door. She stops and turns*) You know there's one thing I have always wanted to do, Madame.
Marie What's that?
Therese To go and live in Paris.

Therese opens the door and goes out

Marie looks after her. The implication of the remark goes home, and she crushes the torn pieces of paper in her hands. The Lights fade to a BLACKOUT

SCENE 2

The same. The following morning

The stage is empty. The door to the children's room is open and we hear the chatter of Celeste and Helene off. They are excited. Miss Clay comes into the room during the following

Miss Clay (*as she enters*) Celeste, will you stop jumping up and down on your case like that. You'll break the hinges.
Celeste (*off*) When is Papa coming?
Miss Clay He'll be here any minute. (*She moves to the Marquise's room and knocks on the door*)
Miss Clay Madame la Marquise...(*Pause*) Madame...
Marie (*off*) Yes, Miss Clay?

Act II Scene 2   45

Miss Clay The children seem to have acquired two of your handkerchiefs. I was wondering whether you'd like to pack them with your things.
Marie Pack them with the children's clothes, Miss Clay. It doesn't matter.

Miss Clay moves back across the room

Marie opens the door of her room and enters

Miss Clay?
Miss Clay Yes, Madame?
Marie My husband should be here shortly.
Miss Clay Any moment, I imagine, Madame.
Marie Well, Miss Clay, when he does arrive, I'd be grateful if—if you wouldn't allow the children to talk about the—the incident...
Miss Clay The photographer, Madame?
Marie Yes—the photographer. I wouldn't want my husband to think the incident had upset me. It has, of course, but I wouldn't want him to think it had. I mean the holiday was spoilt enough by his departure on business, and it would make him feel wretched to think that another incident had spoiled it even more...
Miss Clay I quite understand, Madame.
Marie Oh, and Miss Clay—er—I'm expecting Mademoiselle Paul to call on me before I leave...
Miss Clay Mademoiselle Paul?
Marie Yes. Yes. I—er—said I'd help her a little—you know, financially. It's the least I can do...
Miss Clay That's very generous of you, Madame.
Marie Yes. Well, when she comes I'd like to see her—whatever I may be doing at the time—you understand?
Miss Clay Yes, Madame.

Helene rushes into the room with a small bag

Helene Miss Clay—Miss Clay, where shall I put this bag of shells?
Miss Clay (*sniffing*) They smell dreadful, Helene. Don't you think they should be left behind?
Helene Oh, no.
Miss Clay Well, I think they should.
Helene If I have to leave them behind then Celeste must leave her dead starfish behind too.
Miss Clay What? A dead starfish? Where is it? Celeste! Celeste!

Miss Clay takes Helene and goes off

Marie looks round the room and sighs nervously. Off we hear the children arguing about the keeping of the shells and the starfish. We hear Miss Clay remonstrating with them, the noise is too much for Marie. She goes to the door, shuts it and then leans against it closing her eyes. Suddenly there is a gentle knock on the hall door. She becomes nervous. She slowly moves to the door and opens it

Elise stands outside

Marie Oh...

Elise Hello, Marie.

Marie moves away to the balcony

(*Moving into the room*) I've come to say good-bye. (*She closes the door*) I'm leaving today, Marie.

No reply

I don't suppose we shall see each other again.
Marie I think that is more than likely, Elise.
Elise (*moving forward*) I know you hate me for what I said to you...
Marie I don't want to talk about it. I want to forget it.
Elise You may find that very difficult...
Marie (*coldly*) Maybe. Maybe not.
Elise I feel sorry for you.
Marie (*turning to face her*) Do you? Do you really? I don't see why. I have so much. Others have so little. You allow my outward appearance to deceive you, Elise. I'm quite hard inside, you know. (*She moves towards the chaise-longue*)
Elise I hope everything turns out well for you.

Marie sits down, does not respond. Elise moves and sits down beside Marie

Marie...
Marie Yes.
Elise I will not try and advise you what to do...
Marie I'm pleased about that.
Elise But allow me to suggest one thing.
Marie What?
Elise You cannot go on living with this on your mind. It will destroy you. You will have to tell someone. You will have to tell your husband.
Marie (*standing and moving away*) Never. I will never tell Edouard. And you're wrong, Elise. I can live with it. I did not—murder—Monsieur Paul, whatever you think. It was an accident. The police think it was an accident.
Elise How do you know?
Marie What?
Elise You seem so sure. About what the police think.
Marie Mademoiselle Paul told me yesterday. She said the police are convinced it was an accident.
Elise The papers didn't say so.
Marie The papers print what they'd *like* the police to think. The police think it was an accident. And they are right. It was an accident.
Elise Then why don't you tell the police precisely that? Bring it out in the open, Marie—that's all—clear the air.
Marie Because there is no need. There is no need to tell them what they already know and what Mademoiselle Paul already knows. Neither is there any need to hurt my family any further. And I warn you, Elise. Should you at any time voice the opinion to anyone that the death of that photographer was anything else but an accident, then I shall be forced to take legal action.
Elise (*taken aback*) I believe you would...

Act II Scene 2   47

Marie Yes. I would. I trust I make my position crystal clear.
Elise You have made your position perfectly clear, Marie.
Marie Good, I'm pleased.
Elise You can rest assured, Marie, that I shall try—as soon as I can—to forget this unhappy fortnight.
Marie I'd be grateful if you would.
Elise The biggest regret I have is that our renewed acquaintance has been so short lived.
Marie I regret that too, Elise. But life is like that, isn't it?
Elise (*near to tears*) No, Marie. Not always. (*Stands*) Well, I'll say good-bye then.
Marie If you would. I still haven't completed my packing and Edouard should be here any minute. He's journeying down from Paris. I thought it was very kind and considerate of him.
Elise (*edged with sarcasm*) Yes. You're very lucky—to have such a kind and considerate husband. Good-bye, Marie.
Marie Good-bye, Elise.

Elise moves to the door. Marie does not even look round

> *At the door, Elise turns and takes one more look at Marie, then goes out. After a pause, Marie turns and goes into her bedroom. At the same moment Celeste and Helene enter from their room, followed by Miss Clay*

Celeste Mama!
Helene Papa's here—Papa's here...
Celeste Papa's here...

The door opens and Marie comes out

Miss Clay It's true, Madame. Monsieur le Marquis has just arrived. We saw him from the window coming up the drive.
Marie Oh, that's wonderful...
Helene Can we go down to meet him?
Celeste ⎱ Please, Mama...   ⎰ *Speaking*
Helene ⎰ Oh please, Mama...   ⎱ *together*
Marie All right. All right. But don't make such a noise about it. I think the other guests will be delighted when we've gone. Take them down, Miss Clay, otherwise we won't hear ourselves think.
Miss Clay Very well, Madame.
Helene (*hurrying to the door*) Come on, Celeste.
Marie Quietly girls. Quietly.
Celeste Yes, Mama.
Helene Sorry, Mama.

Helene and Celeste open the hall door

> *Therese stands on the threshold, about to knock*

Miss Clay (*taken aback*) Oh, Mademoiselle Paul... (*To the children*) Er—run along children—quickly.

Therese stands aside

Helene and Celeste exit quickly

Therese May I come in?

Miss Clay turns to see if Marie has seen Therese: she has

Marie Yes, Mademoiselle Paul. Please do.

Therese comes into the room

Miss Clay I won't be long, Madame.

Miss Clay exits

Marie My husband's just arrived. They've gone to meet him.
Therese I came just in time then. Before you left.
Marie Yes. I'll get the money. Excuse me.

Marie hurries into the bedroom

Therese goes to the balcony and looks out towards the headland

Marie hurries back into the room with some notes and stops when she sees Therese on the balcony, then goes to her

Here you are.
Therese A beautiful view, Madame.
Marie Yes.
Therese You can actually see the headland from here.

Therese turns round, moves towards Marie and takes the small bundle of notes

Marie There's twenty thousand francs there. I hope that's sufficient.
Therese For now, Madame. For now. I—er—don't appear to have your address in Paris.
Marie I've put my card in with the money.

Therese begins to check

You have my word on it, Mademoiselle.
Therese I expect you want me to leave before your husband arrives.
Marie Please.
Therese Very well. I will be in communication with you, Madame.
Marie Of that I have no doubt. What will you do? Write? Telephone?
Therese (*with underlying menace*) I'll call on you, I expect. To pay my respects. To see if you and the children are well. May I wish you a pleasant journey home, Madame la Marquise, and happy memories of your holiday, and—above all—no regrets. Good day.

Therese goes to the door

It opens, and Edouard enters

Marie, panic-stricken, hurries to his arms

Marie Edouard! Oh, Edouard darling...(*She kisses his cheek*)
Edouard Marie, my dear. (*Seeing Therese, he becomes slightly embarrassed at Marie's display of affection*) I didn't know you had a visitor.

Act II   Scene 2

Marie It'll take ages to explain but something has happened. An accident—a dreadful accident...
Edouard Will you introduce me, Marie?
Marie Oh, sorry, Edouard. Of course.
Therese Please do not trouble. I'm just leaving and I'm in rather a hurry. Good day, Monsieur le Marquis. Good day, Madame.
Marie Good day, Mademoiselle Paul.

Therese hobbles out

Edouard stares at her as she goes

Edouard Who on earth was that?
Marie Oh, Edouard, hold me. Please. Please hold me...

Edouard holds her in his arms

Edouard What's the matter, my dear? You're trembling.
Marie I'm so pleased to see you. I've missed you so much.
Edouard I know. I'm sorry. But the whole business became so complicated. How you must hate me...
Marie No, my darling. I don't hate you. I love you.
Edouard I've ruined your holiday.
Marie I forgive you.
Edouard I won't ever let it happen again.
Marie Please don't, Edouard. I missed you terribly. I was so lonely...
Edouard I'm sorry, Marie.

Marie breaks away from him

Marie Where are the children, Edouard? Miss Clay?
Edouard Oh, they met a man in the hotel lounge. They seemed to know him quite well. Miss Clay whispered to me that he was a Lord.
Marie Oh, that's right. He invited the children on to his yacht for tea.
Edouard A yacht indeed? Miss Clay's aiming a little high, isn't she?
Marie Come and sit down for a moment.

They move to the chaise-longue

Edouard It's not so hot today.
Marie I think the weather's breaking.
Edouard Some heavy clouds building up.
Marie (*sitting*) Are we in for a storm, do you think?
Edouard (*sitting*) It's possible. You look tired, my darling. Your eyes are red. Have you been crying?
Marie Never mind about me. Oh, Edouard, it's so good having you here...
Edouard Who was that woman?
Marie I never thought I'd miss anyone...
Edouard Who was she, Marie?
Marie Mademoiselle Paul?
Edouard If that's her name. Yes.
Marie She's the sister of the little photographer.

Edouard You mean the one who was going to take our family portrait?
Marie Yes. That's right.
Edouard So what was she doing here?
Marie Well, my dear, soon after he took the photographs of the children and me he was up on the headland—photographing the birds I gather—he trod too near the edge and fell. He was a cripple like his sister. They only found the body yesterday.
Edouard How dreadful for you.
Marie Yes it was a shock and I haven't really got over it. He was a nice young man. Very polite. And a very good photographer. But it seems his sister is now destitute.
Edouard And I suppose she came here begging for money and you, being the kind person you are, gave her everything in your purse.
Marie Well, Edouard, I thought I'd try and help. You see we have so much and they—well, they have so little. As it is she's going to have to sell their photographic business. She's even talking about coming to Paris.
Edouard Oh?
Marie Yes.
Edouard How did the photographs turn out?
Marie What dear?
Edouard The pictures of you and the children.
Marie Oh—I never saw them, come to think of it.
Edouard You never saw them?
Marie No. He hadn't developed them before he was killed.
Edouard How unfortunate. I hear you've been doing a lot of walking while I've been away.
Marie How did you know?
Edouard Miss Clay mentioned it when I phoned on several occasions and you weren't here. You seemed to be walking somewhere every day.
Marie Oh, there's something I must tell you. I met an old school friend. You've heard me talk of Elise.
Edouard No.
Marie I must have mentioned her to you. She was here. Staying in the same hotel. Haven't seen her for twenty years. Isn't that a remarkable coincidence?

Edouard rises

Where are you going?
Edouard To phone reception. Ask them to send up a porter for our valises. I take it you're all packed.
Marie I believe so. Oh, Edouard, before you do that...
Edouard Yes, dear?

A distant clap of thunder is heard

There. I told you. We're going to have a storm.

The light in the room starts to turn grey

(*Thoughtfully*) Strange...

Act II Scene 2

Marie What, dear?
Edouard Oh, I was thinking of that woman who was here just now...
Marie You said strange.
Edouard Nothing strange about *her* as such, Marie. Strange that both she and her brother should be deformed like that.
Marie Oh? It hadn't crossed my mind.
Edouard It often runs in families that's all. That's why it struck me. Reminds me of an old friend of mine.

Another clap of thunder. The room darkens

Marie What do you mean?
Edouard You've never met Richard du Boulay have you? He was crippled, much the same as this unfortunate little photographer of yours and his sister. But for all that, a charming, perfectly normal woman fell in love with him and they eventually married. A son was born and unfortunately he turned out to have a hopeless club foot just like his father. That sort of thing isn't confined to the working classes you see...

Marie slowly pulls away from Edouard. A look of inner horror overtakes her at the thought of the deformed child she herself could be carrying. Her hands clasp her stomach. She feels physically sick

You can't fight that sort of thing. It's a taint in the blood that's passed on.
Marie Edouard?
Edouard What on earth's the matter, Marie? (*Looking at her*) I'm sorry. I shouldn't have spoken of such things. It was thoughtless of me. I think we better go home. I'll phone and get the valises taken down.
Marie Yes—yes, please do that, Edouard.

Edouard goes to the phone. Marie sits quite still

Edouard (*on the phone*) Hello...Ah, yes...Would you send a porter straight away please...Room one-oh-four...Our valises need taking down... Thank you. (*He replaces the receiver and turns. He sighs heavily*) I don't think we'll come back here again. We need a change.
Marie Edouard?
Edouard (*moving to her*) Yes, my dear?
Marie What you just said.
Edouard You must forget what I said. That kind of thing only happens to one person in a thousand—in a million, even.
Marie A taint in the blood you say?
Edouard (*sitting beside her*) That's right.
Marie Inherited, you say?
Edouard Yes.

Marie puts her head on his shoulder and closes her eyes in fear

Marie—Marie, are you all right?
Marie Yes—yes...
Edouard We're going home to Paris. You'll be safe in Paris. Quite safe.

More thunder. Rain begins to spatter on the balcony
Marie (*fearfully*) Safe, Edouard? Did you say—safe?
There is another clap of thunder, and the room grows darker, as—
> the CURTAIN slowly falls

FURNITURE AND PROPERTY LIST

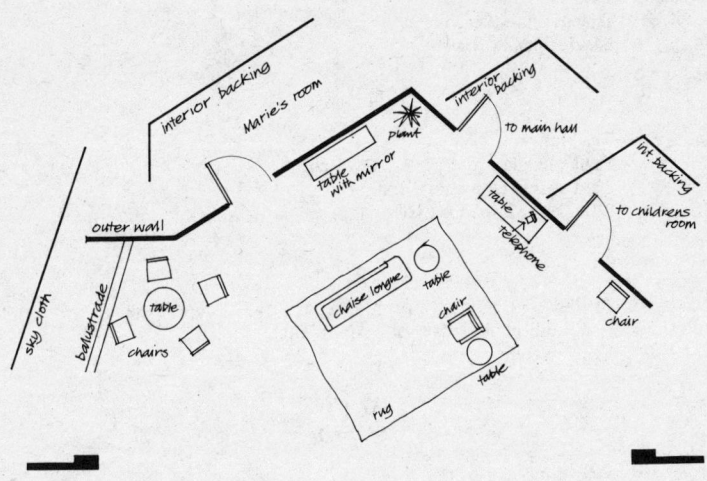

ACT I

Scene 1

On stage: ROOM:
    Chaise-longue
    Matching armchair
    Small chair
    Chiffonier. *Above it:* mirror
    Table. *On it:* telephone
    2 small ornate tables
    Pedestal plant or ornament
    Rug
    Key in **Marie**'s bedroom door

    BALCONY:
    Circular table. *On it:* covered tray with coffee pot, milk jug, sugar bowl, 2 cups, 2 saucers, 2 spoons, 2 small plates, 2 knives, plate of croissants, butter dish, butter knife
    4 small chairs
    Potted plants

Off stage: Briefcase (**Edouard**)
    Tray with coffee pot, milk jug, sugar bowl, 2 cups, 2 saucers, 2 spoons (**Waiter**)

Scene 2

Strike:	Coffee things
Off stage:	Tripod camera with cloth, box of plates (**Paul**) Tray with teapot, milk jug, sugar bowl, 2 cups, 2 saucers, 2 spoons (**Waiter**)
Personal:	**Celeste:** handkerchief **Helene:** handkerchief **Marie:** pendant watch

Scene 3

Strike:	Tea things
Set:	**Paul**'s camera and plate box in corner **Paul**'s jacket on chaise-longue
Off stage:	2 buckets, 2 spades (**Miss Clay**)

Scene 4

Off stage:	Trolley with teapot, milk jug, sugar bowl, 2 cups, 2 saucers, 2 spoons, 2 small plates, plate of cake (**Waiter**)
Personal:	**Elise:** watch

ACT II
Scene 1

Strike:	Tea things
Off stage:	500 franc note (**Marie**) Envelope containing photographs (**Therese**)

Scene 2

Off stage:	Bag of sea-shells (**Helene**) Bundle of franc notes and card (**Marie**)

LIGHTING PLOT

Property fittings required: nil
Interior. An hotel room. The same scene throughout

ACT I Scene 1 Morning
To open: General effect of hot sunshine
Cue 1:   **Marie:** "... the girls and I."   (Page 10)
             Fade to BLACKOUT

ACT I Scene 2 Afternoon
To open: Effect of golden afternoon sunshine
Cue 2:   **Paul:** "Tomorrow, then."   (Page 22)
             Fade to BLACKOUT

ACT I Scene 3 Afternoon
To open: As previous scene
Cue 3:   **Elise:** "... must *never* be weak."   (Page 27)
             Fade to BLACKOUT

ACT I Scene 4 Afternoon
To open: As previous scene
No cues

ACT II Scene 1 Morning
To open: As Act I Scene 1
Cue 4:   **Marie** crushes photographs   (Page 44)
             Fade to BLACKOUT

ACT II Scene 2 Morning
To open: As previous scene
Cue 5:   **Edouard:** "We're going to have a storm."   (Page 50)
             Lighting gradually turns grey as storm approaches
Cue 6:   **Edouard:** "... an old friend of mine."   (Page 51)
             Room darkens further
Cue 7:   **Marie:** "Did you say—safe?"   (Page 52)
             A further darkening as CURTAIN *falls*

EFFECTS PLOT

ACT I
Scene 1

Cue 1:	As Curtain rises *Distant sound of sea: fade as dialogue starts*	(Page 1)
Cue 2:	**Marie** returns from balcony *Telephone rings*	(Page 3)
Cue 3:	**Waiter** moves to balcony *Telephone rings*	(Page 6)

Scene 2

Cue 4:	**Marie:** "... blinded by their own pride." *Telephone rings*	(Page 13)

Scene 3

Cue 5:	As Curtain rises *Telephone rings: stops as* **Miss Clay** *goes to pick up receiver: restarts as she is about to exit: stops after she exits*	(Page 22)
Cue 6:	**Elise:** "... can remain intact ..." *Telephone rings*	(Page 27)

Scene 4

Cue 7:	**Helene** (off) "Yes, Miss Clay." *Telephone rings*	(Page 28)
Cue 8:	**Marie:** "... this wouldn't have happened ..." *Telephone rings*	(Page 33)
Cue 9:	**Marie:** "... telephone would stop." *Telephone stops*	(Page 33)

ACT II
Scene 1

Cue 10:	**Elise** rises after **Marie**'s exit *Telephone rings*	(Page 38)

Scene 2

Cue 11:	**Edouard:** "Yes, dear?" *Distant clap of thunder*	(Page 50)
Cue 12:	**Edouard:** "... an old friend of mine." *Clap of thunder*	(Page 51)
Cue 13:	**Edouard:** "Quite safe." *Thunder. Rain*	(Page 51)
Cue 14:	**Marie:** "Did you say—safe?" *Thunder*	(Page 52)

Printed in Great Britain by Butler & Tanner Ltd, Frome and London